Hong Kong in China

EAI Occasional Paper No. 18

Hong Kong in China
Perspectives from the Region

edited by

Andrew M. MARTON

EAST ASIAN INSTITUTE
National University of Singapore

World Scientific
Singapore • New Jersey • London • Hong Kong

SINGAPORE UNIVERSITY PRESS
NATIONAL UNIVERSITY OF SINGAPORE

Published by
World Scientific Publishing Co. Pte. Ltd.
P O Box 128, Farrer Road, Singapore 912805
USA office: Suite 1B, 1060 Main Street, River Edge, NJ 07661
UK office: 57 Shelton Street, Covent Garden, London WC2H 9HE
and
Singapore University Press Pte. Ltd.
Yusof Ishak House, National University of Singapore
10 Kent Ridge Crescent, Singapore 119260

HONG KONG IN CHINA: PERSPECTIVES FROM THE REGION
EAI Occasional Paper No. 18

Copyright © 1999 by World Scientific Publishing Co. Pte. Ltd. and
Singapore University Press Pte. Ltd.

All rights reserved. This book, or parts thereof, may not be reproduced in any form or by any means, electronic or mechanical, including photocopying, recording or any information storage and retrieval system now known or to be invented, without written permission from the Publishers.

For photocopying of material in this volume, please pay a copying fee through the Copyright Clearance Center, Inc., 222 Rosewood Drive, Danvers, MA 01923, USA. In this case permission to photocopy is not required from the publishers.

ISBN 981-02-4103-0 (pbk)

Printed in Singapore.

FOREWORD

The East Asian Institute (EAI) is an autonomous research organization established in April 1997 under a statute of the National University of Singapore. It is the successor of the former Institute of East Asian Political Economy (IEAPE). The mission of the EAI is to undertake research on a wide range of topics including the regional and global impact of a resurgent People's Republic of China, its political and social changes as a result of recent dynamic economic growth, the quest for cultural rejuvenation among the Chinese people, cultural and commercial networks of the ethnic Chinese from a global perspective, and developments in Hong Kong, Taiwan and Macao. The EAI also monitors political, economic and social trends in China and seeks to promote empirical and policy-oriented research based on sound scholarship. To promote scholarly exchange and to enable its research findings to reach wider public and academic audiences, the EAI holds regular seminars and publishes a series of background briefs, working papers and occasional papers, and organizes regional and international conferences and workshops on East Asian issues.

The chapters which appear in this volume were originally presented at the *Conference on Hong Kong in China: A Year Later* held in Singapore, 29–31 October 1998 and hosted by the East Asian Institute. The conference included an array of presentations on Hong Kong's transition since 1 July 1997 in the fields of economics, politics, law, and social changes. Revised versions of these papers will appear in a companion volume titled **Hong Kong in China: The Challenges of Transition** jointly edited by Professors Wang Gungwu and John

Wong (Singapore: Times Academic Press). In addition to these contributions, a number of papers were also presented in two special sessions on *Hong Kong and Greater China* and *Hong Kong and the Region*. The contributions included in this volume, edited by Dr. Andrew M. Marton, were selected from these latter two sessions. While the issues addressed in these papers were clearly linked to the wider themes of the conference, taken together they were substantive and distinct enough to be considered viable as a separate book-length EAI Occasional Paper.

May 1999   Professor Wang Gungwu
Director

ACKNOWLEDGEMENTS

The editor wishes to express his gratitude to Professor John Wong for inviting him to participate in the conference and for the opportunity to edit these proceedings. A special note of thanks is due to the EAI Research Officers, Messrs. WONG Chee Kong, TAM Chen Hee, GU Qingyang and Miss CUI Wei who prepared summaries of each paper and who endured with considerable fortitude and good humour their roles as rapporteurs. I also wish to convey my appreciation to the authors of each chapter, and to the respective discussants for their written comments, all of whom participated enthusiastically in the editorial process. Responsibility for errors of interpretation remains that of the individual authors. The views expressed in each chapter are solely those of the authors and not those of their respective institutions. Errors arising from the editing process are the sole responsibility of the editor.

May 1999 Dr. Andrew M. Marton
Research Fellow

CONTENTS

Foreword	v
Acknowledgments	vii
Introduction: Regional Perspectives on Hong Kong's Transition to China *Andrew M. MARTON*	1
Hong Kong in China: Partnership as a New Pattern of Relations *GAO Shangquan*	15
Taiwan in Transition: Adjusting to the New Reality of One Country Two Systems *Milton D. YEH*	25
The Challenge of "*San Tong*" for Hong Kong *LUO Qi*	42
Hong Kong's Transition: A View from Indonesia *Jusuf WANANDI*	64
Hong Kong's Transition: A View from Malaysia *Stephen LEONG*	75
Hong Kong's Transition: A View from Thailand *UMPHON Phanachet*	91
Hong Kong's Transition: A View from the South Pacific *Gerald CHAN*	104
Contributors	131

INTRODUCTION: REGIONAL PERSPECTIVES ON HONG KONG'S TRANSITION TO CHINA

Andrew M. MARTON

The period since Hong Kong's return to Chinese sovereignty on 1 July 1997 has coincided with the emergence of a number of circumstances which have deeply affected both places and the region. Thus, while China and Hong Kong must grapple with the special challenges of a transition that is quite unique to their own experience, they are also caught up in the pervasive and highly dynamic developments reshaping the wider Asia-Pacific region.[1] Conversely, it is also possible to argue that Hong Kong's reversion also comes at a point in history when overall circumstances are much improved (despite nagging new problems) compared to the middle of the 19th Century when China was forced to cede the territory. In this context, it is interesting to note that much of the debate since the signing of the Joint Declaration in 1984, and

---

[1] See for example: Severance, J. (1997) Hong Kong's reversion to Chinese sovereignty and its impact on "Greater China": A conference summary. *Pacific Rim Report*, 4 (July).

running through the post-handover period, has focused primarily on the relatively localized political, social, cultural and economic issues of Hong Kong as a part of China. Much less scholarly attention has been devoted to undertaking an analysis and synthesis of particular regional points of view of the transfer of sovereignty. The objective of this volume, therefore, is to compile an array of observations and perceptions on Hong Kong's transition to China since the handover from several perspectives around the Asia-Pacific region.

Prior to the handover, many observers expressed deep concerns about the political future of the SAR under Chinese sovereignty. While much of the underlying unease has not dissipated, the general consensus is that Beijing has largely kept to its promises to uphold a high degree of autonomy and has allowed Hong Kong to retain its *laissez-faire* capitalist system. In fact, circumstances since the handover reveal that while the political transition has been unexpectedly smooth, many are less sanguine about the deep economic downturn and the efficacy and appropriateness of certain responses from the government. However, rather than simply listing the sequence of events in Hong Kong and around the region since 1 July 1997,[2] it would be useful to summarize three interconnected themes which provide a context for the regional perspectives conveyed in this volume.[3]

The first relates to the problems and prospects for economic transformation since the handover. The current unanticipated economic slump has been linked to both external and internal factors which point up some of the structural problems in Hong Kong's economy including the Hong Kong dollar's peg to the U.S.

---

[2] For the most recent chronological survey and analysis of these events see: Chow, L. C. H. & Fan, Y. K. (1999) *The Other Hong Kong Report 1998*. Hong Kong: Chinese University Press.

[3] These themes are drawn from a series of papers delivered at the *Conference on Hong Kong in China: A year later*. Singapore, October 29–31, 1998; and *ibid*.

dollar, the over-reliance on real estate and related investments, the hollowing out of the manufacturing sector to China, and concerns about the development of human resources. Other elements of this theme more directly relevant for the wider region include Hong Kong's shifting role as a gateway and business bridge to China and its critical intermediary role for economic linkages between Taiwan and the Mainland. Hong Kong's short- and long-term responses to the Asian financial crisis and other non-crisis economic imperatives are also important. The government's intervention in the market, for example, has had implications for notions of economic management around the region. Moreover, new policies to stimulate the development of higher value added sectors, and the fact that Hong Kong is simultaneously becoming more economically integrated with China, even as the mainland becomes increasingly less reliant on the SAR for certain functions which link the Chinese economy to the rest of the world, has important implications for the region. Thus, there is a growing sense that Hong Kong will begin to look more closely at its other partners around the region in addition to its conventional focus on China.

The second theme relates to political and legal developments. Clearly, the SAR is still groping for ways to establish a workable and efficient political framework whereby Hong Kong people will gradually learn to govern themselves.[4] Consensus on the general good quality of the administration is not matched by a similar level of popular legitimacy and accountability. The unique phenomenon of an extended period of transition from colony to absorption by another sovereign underlies both the stability and challenges Hong Kong faces today. A high degree of autonomy does not mean

---

[4] Chow, L. C. H. & Fan, Y. K. (1999) "Introduction: The first year of Hong Kong as a Chinese Special Administrative Region". In Chow, L. C. H. & Fan, Y. K. op. cit., p. xxxv.

independence. Thus, much sensitivity and balance is required between the need to recognize the reality of a sovereign China and the implementation of "two systems". In terms of legal culture, for example, there is a tension between maintaining previous structures and the need to invoke meaningful change. In addition to profound self-interest, the way in which such tensions are negotiated and resolved will in part stem from international assistance, pressures and perceptions. The demonstration effect for Taiwan is a key element in this regard. Moreover, Hong Kong's formal participation in regional and international bodies, and its articulation with the wider processes of globalization, ensures that the SAR will endeavour to retain the integrity and the most important attributes of a distinct set of political and legal structures in the eyes of its neighbours.

The third theme has to do with issues of Hong Kong's ostensible Chinese identity. It turns out that one of the most significant transitions in Hong Kong relates not to sovereignty, but to attempts to mould a new identity. The nature of the way Hong Kong Chinese define themselves is embedded within broader questions of nationalism and values, and has implications for the sociological aspects of cultural integration and affinity with the Mainland. These issues are played out in the sometimes messy practical realities of family ties and reunification, as the recent controversy surrounding right of abode amply demonstrates. The high profile phenomenon of emigration overseas introduces an international dimension which adds to the complexity of the identity labyrinth. This is nowhere more clearly highlighted in the tensions between moral authenticity — the individual commitment to being Chinese, Hong Konger, Cantonese, overseas Chinese, or Australian for example — and cosmopolitan hybridity — adopting multiple identities. Acknowledging the full complexity of this tension is relevant from a regional perspective because of the community of Hong Kong born emigrants who, while they may have shifted their place of residence or citizenship, fundamentally retain their Hong Kong identity and interests. The socio-economic and cultural interactions and linkages they bring to their new milieu cannot be ignored.

Overall, it seems that the "big" concerns about democracy, political legitimacy, Hong Kong's autonomy, human rights, rule of law and other fears relating to the handover have either not materialized or have faded into the background. Instead, much more grounded and grassroots issues have emerged as more important, stemming in part from the unexpected impact of the Asian financial crisis and other more localized events referred to throughout the rest of this volume. The interrelated themes as they have been highlighted here, are meant to provide a preliminary context for understanding and positioning each of the regional perspectives portrayed in the following chapters.

The first chapter, a short essay from Gao, explores the notion of a new "partnership" between the Hong Kong SAR and China to explain the particular patters of relations which have emerged since the transition. Gao's analysis is embedded in the official Chinese interpretation of events since 1 July 1997. Most views of the one country two systems formula highlight the institutional arrangements which seek to bridge or reconcile the differences between China and Hong Kong. Gao suggests that this perspective under emphasizes the nature of the precise interactions and interrelationships between both sides which are characterized by increasing interdependence, particularly in economic terms. Conceptualizing the relationship between Hong Kong and China as a partnership allows for an analysis of the underlying complexities and dynamics of interactions between the two.

Thus, while there is much within the one country two systems arrangement as it was originally conceived by Deng Xiaoping that is conventionally viewed as contradictory, the contribution from Gao proposes an alternative perspective. For example, the most obvious "contradiction" between capitalism and socialism has been dispelled since they co-exist and are co-developing within one country. Moreover, the sometimes awkward ideological and administrative mechanisms invoked to accommodate a capitalist island in a socialist system have, since the transfer of sovereignty, yielded to the practical realities of recognizing, articulating and strengthening common interests. Gao reviews a number of circumstances which have arisen in Hong Kong since 1 July 1997 to illustrate how partnership with China is indicative of this new pattern of relations. As such, Gao provides a necessary point of reference for positioning subsequent chapters which examine Hong Kong's transition from around the region.

The next two chapters from Yeh and Luo provide some insights into the Taiwan perspective of Hong Kong's return to China. The chapter form Yeh focuses primarily upon the politics of the "one China" principle as it is embedded in the one country two systems formula for Hong Kong. Rather than focusing on the situation in Hong Kong *per se*, Yeh introduces an analytical framework for understanding competing notions of the one China principle which emerge from Taiwan and the Mainland. He suggests that it is the internal dynamics of the domestic political structures of both regimes which both determine and endorse different perceptions of one China. While this concept is not new, by setting the analysis against Hong Kong's transition to China, Yeh is able to unpack the underlying political motives of Beijing's one country two systems formula and Taiwan's response.

Yeh begins by establishing the origins of the one China debate and subsequent policy frameworks as they emerged in Taiwan and the Mainland prior to the late 1970s. He clearly links the practice of pursuing notions of one China to the explicit need by the ruling elite on both sides of the strait to maintain political legitimacy. By the early 1980s, and in the context of negotiations between Britain and China leading to the Joint Declaration in 1984, Taiwan was forced to respond to a new Mainland version of one China which accommodated two systems. Taiwan has rejected this reformulation of one China. However, Taiwan has also explicitly and implicitly abandoned much of its "cold war" policy against the Mainland and has simultaneously undertaken a successful process of democratization. This has stimulated, or at least accommodated, alternative visions of Taiwan's relationship to China including independence. Of course, China strongly opposes such alternatives, and according to Yeh, is obviously uneasy about the challenges to its one China vision arising from Taiwan's strengthening democracy. Furthermore, Yeh also suggests that China's specific responses are indicative of the nature of its internal political structures and mechanisms, thereby explicating events such as China's missile tests over the island. Following a similar analytical vein, he also proposes that the formulation and implementation of Taiwanese policies toward the Mainland will be increasing undertaken with reference to public opinion and the electoral process. Therefore, despite the apparent initial success of the handover of Hong Kong to China under the one country two systems formula, Yeh's basic conclusion is that the nature of cross-Straits relations and notions of one China will remain subject primarily to the respective internal politics in Taiwan and the Mainland.

There has been much ado about the one country two systems being originally conceived as a model for Taiwan's reunification with the Mainland. However, as Luo argues in chapter three, Taiwan has observed the post-handover period with considerable interest not because it serves as a model of reunification, but because it has an enormous economic stake in the outcome. Thus, for many in Taiwan the complexities of reunification and cross-Straits relations are separate and secondary to the economic issues. From this perspective, Luo seeks to address several overlapping issues about the nature of Hong Kong's role in as an entrêpot hub for both Taiwan and China. Marshaling the most recent trade data available, he illustrates how China relies on Hong Kong more than does Taiwan as its main gateway to international markets, while Taiwan relies on Hong Kong more than the Mainland as its main conduit for indirect trade with China. Furthermore, while the relative importance of Hong Kong as the main channel for indirect trade between China and the Taiwan declined somewhat in the years immediately preceding 1 July 1997, despite the trauma of the financial crisis, Luo shows that the trends have not been significantly altered since the handover.

These findings provide an important analytical foundation for understanding the potential impact on Hong Kong of a resumption of regular trading and other linkages — the "*san tong*" of Luo's title — between Taiwan and the Mainland. The conclusion reached can be divided into two parts. First, Luo suggests that since Hong Kong will continue as an efficient entrêpot, a significant proportion of the trade between China and Taiwan would be retained should direct links resume. However, he also elaborates on a second parallel scenario whereby the resumption of *san tong* could have a significant impact on China's re-exports to foreign countries. Luo sketches out the political and economic dimensions of a possible diversion of Mainland re-exports to Taiwanese ports. Even though much of this latter analysis is somewhat speculative under the current conditions, it is nevertheless a worthwhile exercise contemplating how such a scenario might impact Hong Kong as both China and Taiwan come closer to WTO accession and the possibility of re-establishing direct trade and other linkages.

The next three chapters from Wanandi, Leong and Umphon report the views on Hong Kong's transition from the three ASEAN countries of Indonesia, Malaysia and Thailand respectively. Each of these chapters have adopted a largely sanguine view of Hong Kong in transition. All of the authors support the notion that Hong Kong has remained politically stable and that Beijing has kept to its promises not to interfere in the SAR. These three chapters from various southeast Asian perspectives separately identify the need to simultaneously implement creative mechanisms to safeguard and nurture Hong Kong's political development while accommodating the realities of a new Chinese sovereign. They all observe, moreover, that while in the eyes of many the handover was not expected to proceed smoothly, Hong Kong was able to respond appropriately to an array of difficult and largely unexpected circumstances. Although the authors have each expressed a limited amount of uncertainty regarding Hong Kong's future as part of China, all have favourably acknowledged recent policy efforts to restructure the local economy and to build upon the important gateway role and investment potential of the SAR for the region. Interestingly, these chapters also refer to evidence which suggests that southeast Asian based trade and investment interests in China are starting to bypass Hong Kong in favour of direct linkages.

Beyond these broadly similar perceptions of the transition, however, each of these three contributions reveals a distinct set of insights stemming in part from the respective geo-political position of each commentator. Thus, Wanandi from an Indonesian perspective emphasizes the politics of good government and the development of effective structures of governance; Leong's view from Malaysia is imbued with sympathetic affinity and relief arising from an array of unexpected events which occurred in Hong Kong since the handover, and; Umphon from Thailand chooses to elaborate on the specific areas of cooperation and complimentarity with Hong Kong including elements of a networked pan-Asian vision.

Although the notions of Chinese sovereignty and the special status of Hong Kong within China have not yet been clearly defined according to Wanandi, he does suggest that the SAR should be given the opportunity to pursue its own meaningful political develoment. He specifically refers to the recent tumultuous events in Indonesia to support his contention that China must not neglect the desire of the people of Hong Kong to maintain and build upon their relatively advanced polity. This view pervades his interpretation of Hong Kong's response to other events since the handover. He is critical of the perceived aloofness of the bureaucratic elite, for example, choosing to highlight how the government should have been able to avoid its massive intervention to stabilize the market in August 1998. In terms of the importance of Hong Kong for the rest of Asia, Wanandi portrays the SAR as a key element in bringing a stable and prosperous China to the regional and international table. Hong Kong's constructive role in regional and international bodies, and its successful participation in the wider processes of globalization — notwithstanding the recent financial turmoil in Asia — should serve as an effective influence on China. Wanandi also refers to Hong Kong as a valuable base for regional intellectual discourse complimenting its important regional and global partnerships. From the Indonesian perspective, Hong Kong can utilize these attributes to negotiate its multiple identities in a context where sovereignty is no longer absolute and the interplay between global and local forces pose new challenges for the SAR as part of a rapidly transforming China.

Chapter 5 from Leong positions the Malaysian view of Hong Kong's transition to China by invoking a common history of colonialism. This establishes the author's interpretation of a Malaysian affinity (and relief) for much that has happened in the SAR since 1 July 1997. His sense of the need for political stability as a basis for economic development, for example, is highlighted in his suspicions regarding the motivation of the last governor to upset the status quo by pressing for democratic reforms. Leong's most interesting insights emerge from his portrayal of the Malaysian response to two key events in Hong Kong since the handover. The first relates to the way in which the deeply problematic opening of the new airport in Hong Kong drew attention away from the difficulties experienced following the opening of the new Kuala Lumpur airport just a few days earlier. The second relates to Malaysia's sympathetic view of the Hong Kong government's market intervention in response to the perceived irresponsibility of international speculators. Leong describes the emergence of a kind of common cause consensus with Hong Kong as he recounts the explicit I-told-you-so tone of calls in Malaysia for a more closely regulated international financial regime. Malaysians were disappointed, however, when the Hong Kong authorities subsequently distanced themselves from such calls. In more general terms, Hong Kong's transition is conceptualized as part of Malaysia's overall relationship with China. Moreover, by acknowledging the supporting role of China during the transition, Leong conveys Malaysian optimism about Hong Kong's inherent ability to adapt and thrive.

Umphon from Thailand begins chapter six with a pragmatic southeast Asian interpretation of post-handover Hong Kong which elaborates on the need for the SAR authorities to address the practical issues of local aspirations for greater democracy and maintaining a competitive business environment. He also tentatively foresees a trend towards socio-economic and political convergence between China and Hong Kong. As a compliment to the previous two chapters which refer to Indonesia's and Malaysia's trade ties through Hong Kong to China, Umphon very much focuses upon the strong trade and investment linkages between the SAR and Thailand. This provides the context for his examination of the prospects for complimentarity and cooperation between Hong Kong and Thailand. He introduces Thailand's unique geo-political role in promoting a pan-Asian network of linked infrastructure for which Hong Kong's experience and expertise as a gateway to China, combined with its potential for investment, would facilitate region-wide prosperity. Umphon also identifies a number of other strategic economic, technological, and human resource related complimentarities. Thus, the Thai view of Hong Kong's transition to China is positioned in terms of a common array of problems and a shared destiny. While structural weaknesses in Hong Kong are acknowledged under this rubric, the SAR's apparent capacity to effectively respond to such challenges, and with the continued support of an appropriately cooperative China, bodes well for the entire region.

The final chapter from Chan focuses on the official Australian and New Zealand government perspectives on Hong Kong's transition. The chapter explores the surprisingly robust linkages between Hong Kong and the antipodes, especially in terms of trade and investments, provision of services including education, migration, and the rather unique phenomenon of Australian and New Zealand involvement in judicial practice in the SAR. Chan's central argument is that despite an ambient level of concern about human rights and good governance, Australian and New Zealand relations with Hong Kong are grounded in the "low politics" of the issues identified above. Chan suggests implicitly that the reasons for this arise from two particular notions. First, Hong Kong is valourized as a cosmopolitan world city within the global arena, and second, both Australia and New Zealand are reassessing their national identities as part of their apparent desire to be "more Asian."

Thus, Chan provides an array of data to establish the strong ties between Hong Kong and Australia and New Zealand. Similar to the other regional perspectives addressed in previous chapters, mutual trade, investments, and market opportunities are again highlighted. In addition to these, however, Chan singles out three further types of linkages not found in these other relationships. Australia and New Zealand together account for significant proportions of the export of services to Hong Kong especially in terms of education, tourism and producer services. The direct movement and exchange of people is also significant. Australia, for example, is one of the most popular destinations for Hong Kong emigrants, while the SAR is home to the largest group of expatriate Australians worldwide. The third and most unique relationship arises from cooperation in judicial governance. Along with the United Kingdom, both new Zealand and Australia, all of whom share common law traditions with Hong Kong, provide a pool of judges (two each) from which at any given time one will sit on the court of final appeal. Taken together these interactions are part of a relatively "low-key," though direct and influential set of relations between Hong Kong and Australia and New Zealand. However, despite the intensity of these linkages and continuing support for all the attributes which underlie a stable and prosperous Hong Kong, Chan also confirms that interactions with the SAR must be considered in terms of the more important Australian and New Zealand relations with China.

The chapters in this volume represent a diverse array of viewpoints from around the Asia-Pacific region on Hong Kong's transition to Chinese rule. While it was necessary as part of the editorial process to streamline and clarify some of the arguments presented, and remaining cognizant of the underlying themes introduced above, the original tone and emphases of each contribution has been preserved. As such, the editor has also deliberately endeavoured to retain the sometimes incompatible and contradictory interpretations of particular events and circumstances. Similarly, much of the apparently inconsistent terminology invoked by the various authors has also not been altered. Thus, China's resumption of sovereignty over Hong Kong is referred to variously as the handover, transition, reunification, return, transfer, reversion, or retrocession among others. This should not distract the reader from the many common perceptions and themes running through the volume. Rather, it merely serves to emphasize the inherent complexities and uncertainties of Hong Kong's transition and the range of alternative regional perspectives which it engenders.

Chapter 1
HONG KONG IN CHINA: PARTNERSHIP AS A NEW PATTERN OF RELATIONS

GAO Shangquan

Introduction

In the period since China resumed sovereignty over Hong Kong a key question has arisen regarding the nature of the relationship between the former British colony and Mainland China. In this chapter I wish to suggest that a new kind of "partnership" has emerged under the rubric of the "one country two systems" formula. The nature of this partnership has come into sharper focus in the context of a number of critical issues that affected not just Hong Kong and China, but the entire region. Some of these issues are explored in the sections which follow particularly in terms of how they have affected Hong Kong in the context of it new partnership with the Mainland. Four overlapping themes will be addressed. The first section will review how the practice of one country two systems has faired in the period since China resumed sovereignty over Hong Kong. The second section will introduce a Mainland perspective on the difficulties and challenges Hong Kong has encountered in the context of the region-wide financial crisis. The third section outlines the Mainland view on the market intervention by the Hong Kong government in response to currency plays in the local market. The analysis here serves to emphasize the need for Hong Kong, China and other Asian countries to ensure the stability of their respective financial markets. The fourth section briefly reviews the context of the relevant macro-reforms in Mainland China and the specific responses implemented since the beginning of the Asian financial crisis particularly as it has affected Hong Kong. The fifth and final section highlights how elements of the newly emerging partnership between Hong Kong and Mainland China serves to strengthen Hong Kong's ability to implement effective strategies for coping with the crisis and to lay the groundwork for future cooperation and mutual benefit.

The Successful Practice of One Country Two Systems in Hong Kong

Since the establishment of the Hong Kong Special Administrative Region (HKSAR) the Chinese government policy of one country two systems, "Hong Kong people ruling Hong Kong" and a "high degree of autonomy," has been successfully implemented. Prior to Hong Kong's return to China, some doubted the one country two systems policy could be realized. It now seems clear that the two different systems of socialism and capitalism can be combined under a single reunified sovereign. While in China socialism is the main system, Hong Kong is carrying out capitalism. That these two systems can co-exist and co-develop is one of the great innovations of Deng Xiaoping theory.

Since the return of Hong Kong, some have remained doubtful about whether or not Beijing would interfere. In order to ensure the full realization of the policy of one country two systems, Hong Kong people ruling Hong Kong and maintaining a high degree of autonomy, the central government has retained a policy of non-interference in any matters of the HKSAR. Everything provided for in the Basic Law, including Hong Kong's capitalist system and the rights of the people of Hong Kong has been practised and has been one hundred percent realized. Hong Kong has maintained its capitalist economic system which is still highly free, highly open and highly internationalized. Moreover, its legal system remains intact such that Hong Kong has independent powers of legislation, administration of justice and final appeal. Hong Kong people have retained their previous life-style — "horses are still racing, people are still dancing, and stocks are still trading." At the first anniversary of Hong Kong's return to China, the first Chief Executive, Mr. Tung Chee Hwa, emphasized in his speech that one country two systems has been successful after one year in practice and that the citizens of Hong Kong are their own real masters. The central government has not interfered in any of Hong Kong's affairs.

However, the central government has also stated many times that whatever the cost, ensuring Hong Kong's stability is most important. This has given the Hong Kong people great encouragement. In April 1998, in the foreword of the report on the issue of Hong Kong submitted by the American administration to the United States Congress, it was clearly stated that there is no evidence showing that the Chinese central government has interfered in any of Hong Kong's local affairs. Even the former Governor of Hong Kong, Mr. Chris Pattern, has acknowledged that since Hong Kong was returned to China, the Chinese leadership has "let the people of Hong Kong rule Hong Kong — there is no more doubt on this issue."

Difficulties and Challenges Faced by Hong Kong Since the Return to Chinese Sovereignty

Under the influence the of Asian financial crisis, Hong Kong has been facing serious difficulties and challenges. International speculators have attacked the fixed exchange rate between the HK dollar and the US dollar via the stock market. In order to defend the pegged exchange rate, inter-bank and other interest rates were significantly increased leading to a sharp decline in the value of the stock market and a decrease in real estate prices. As a result many in Hong Kong have lost some of their property. The overall economy in Hong Kong has also been hit quite hard. Tourism, real estate, retailing and other sectors are in recession, and industrial and trade exports are experiencing difficulties. Some enterprises have had to declare bankruptcy and go into liquidation, laying off employees leading to a significant increase in unemployment. The total value of production in the second quarter of 1998 decreased 5 percent compared with the same period in the previous year. Meanwhile, inflation reached 3.5 percent overall for 1998.

We are confident that the difficulties that Hong Kong is encountering can be overcome. While recognizing the considerable difficulties, we should also look at the favorable conditions which should position Hong Kong well for recovery. For instance, basic economic fundamentals in Hong Kong are still sound and fiscal and foreign reserves are sufficient. Supervision of the financial system is well established. The Hong Kong civil service is well qualified. Hong Kong entrepreneurs are good at trading and management, and have high capacity to adapt to the changes of the international market. Hong Kong is still recognized as one of the most competitive places worldwide. According to a survey by the World Economic Forum reported in June 1998, Hong Kong competitiveness was ranked second among the 53 countries and regions investigated, just after Singapore, but higher than the United States, the United Kingdom and Canada.

A Policy of Non-Intervention Does Not Mean No Concern

Since the outbreak of the Asian crisis in mid-1997, the HK dollar peg has been attacked four times by international speculators. They discovered and proceeded to manipulate a complex idiosyncrasy in the Hong Kong financial system to attack the fixed HK dollar exchange rate. They were selling HK dollars at the currency exchange market while they were simultaneously selling short on listings in the futures and stock markets. They treated Hong Kong as their own automatic money machine. In response to such unacceptable circumstances, the HKSAR mobilized its considerable foreign reserves to intervene in the market.

Critics from different sectors believed that the HKSAR's intervention would damage the hard earned image of Hong Kong as a free and open market and that this would also have a negative impact on public confidence in Hong Kong's financial administrative system. However, supporters believed firstly, that the HKSAR's intervention did not betray a policy of non-intervention, arguing that a free market did not mean absolutely no intervention. There is no absolutely free market anywhere. While we must let the market play its role, if it is subject to distortion or manipulation, it is the responsibility of the government to respond. In the 1980s and 1990s, when the value of the US dollar was declining, the US Federal Reserve propped up the dollar very often in the market. Similarly, inflation is often controlled in the US by adjusting interest rates. Secondly, the aim of the government's appropriate intervention was to stop international speculators from manipulating the market and to protect Hong Kong's economic interests. The desire to maintain a "free economy" should not be outweighed by the "freedom" of international speculators to attack the HK dollar peg by manipulating loopholes in the financial system. Thirdly, the strategy of intervention adopted by the Hong Kong authorities not only minimized the potential losses, but also, more importantly, served to restore the confidence of Hong Kong people and investors in the local markets. As long as the Hong Kong market remains free and a place for profit-making, investors will come like the tide. However, if the financial market is manipulated by international speculators who distort the normal operation of the free market, then investors will hesitate to come.

According to the Basic Law, the HKSAR does not adopt a foreign exchange control policy. This does not mean that the government is not concerned about the exchange rate. With economic globalization and the development of financial derivatives, the full application of advanced information technologies, the global financial system has witnessed an increased movement of international capital. In order to manage the risk caused by the free movement of such vast amounts of capital, and the possible risk of market manipulation caused by international speculators, the HKSAR has adopted 30 different new rules and measures for the market to minimize potential instability in the stock market. These events have also demonstrated the determination of the HKSAR to retain the fixed exchange rate peg and to maintain the stability of its financial market. The measures adopted have played a very important positive role in preventing international speculators from controlling the Hong Kong market helping to avoiding economic losses. Such an initiative has been widely supported by the people of Hong Kong. The most urgent thing now is to develop and implement new international financial rules to regulate the international flow of currency movements to prevent turmoil and speculative profit taking from developing countries.

In this context, I strongly support the measures undertaken by the HKSAR to stabilize its financial market. In 1996, as the economy group leader for the Hong Kong Special Administrative Region Preparatory Committee, I submitted a research report titled *How to Adopt the Lessons From the Mexican and European Monetary Crisis to Ensure the Stability of the Hong Kong Financial Market*. In that report, I pointed out that Southeast Asian countries with large and increasing current account deficits and political instability would become the target of international currency speculators. I also suggested that those international speculators might also use the fixed exchange rate between the HK and US dollars to attack the HK dollar and that the Chinese government, Hong Kong, and other Asian authorities must be alert and prepared for such an offensive. Effective measures must be taken to fight back any speculators who dared to come to the market with ill intent and to make them pay heavily or be aware of the difficulties. I went on to say that Hong Kong would need to increase and be prepared to mobilize the necessary foreign reserves, and to rationally reconfigure the structure of its foreign currency reserves. Meanwhile, as I claimed in the report, it would be very important to coordinate such responses with other initiatives to establish preventive and remedial measures, which, if needed, could be implemented to intervene in the market with strength.

I am, therefore, pleased to see that barely one-year after the return of Hong Kong to Chinese sovereignty, the HKSAR has been able to implement such an effective intervention in the market in response to such urgent conditions. These events, moreover, serve to emphasize the ability of Hong Kong people to rule Hong Kong. I believe that the HKSAR was forced to intervene under the circumstances and did so effectively. Only after some semblance of normality returned to the Hong Kong financial system, wherein speculators were no longer controlling the market, will intervention no longer be necessary.

The Motherland Provides Strong Support for Hong Kong

China has undertaken a series of measures to deepen the reforms, reduce government bureaucracy, reorganize the financial system, adjust economic structures, enhance the basic structure of the investment environment, further develop domestic demand, and increase exports. China has a surplus in its international balance payments and the RMB will remain stable. The strengthening economy of Mainland China should be able to provide effective support for the Hong Kong economy. Whatever the cost, the central government will continue to assist the HKSAR to adopt relevant measures to maintain the stability and development of finance and the economy, positively support Hong Kong's enterprises to invest in Mainland China, develop tourism, high-tech enterprises and the construction of basic infrastructure, develop transshipment trade, the exchange of technology and international cooperation. We are confident that Hong Kong people will be able to make the best use of their own advantages to overcome the current temporary difficulties to further develop their economy.

During the Asian crisis, while some countries have seen their currencies devalue one after another, the Chinese RMB has also encountered pressures to devalue. However, the Chinese government has indicated many times that RMB will not be devalued. This is because China's macro-economy continues its stable development. Although economic growth has slowed somewhat, it is still growing and prices remain relatively stable. Also, China's balance of international payments remain favourable along with its sizable foreign reserves. Although there are pressures on exports, the cost of labor in the exporting sectors is still lower than Southeast Asian countries. Moreover, about 50% of China's exports are actually further processed products imported for this purpose. As such, they are not as affected by the exchange rate. Maintaining a stable RMB exchange rate is a significant contribution to the economic stability of Hong Kong and to the whole world.

Conclusion: Partnership as the Future Pattern of Relations between Hong Kong and the Mainland

The Asian financial crisis has created severe difficulties for the Hong Kong economy. However, it has also provided opportunities for the people of Hong Kong. In the past few years, the steep increases of real estate prices and salaries, combined with continuously high inflation has created a bubble economy in Hong Kong. This has been a great threat to Hong Kong's economic development. The impact of the Asian crisis has deepened the recognition of a need for a readjustment of Hong Kong's economic structure in order to help the economy recover.

According to the characteristics of Hong Kong's economic structure and the economic development trends of the Asia Pacific region, in the context of the present situation and existing problems, the HKSAR needs to consider a long-term agenda for the direction of the Hong Kong economy. First, it seems clear that the services sector will likely remain the key component of Hong Kong's economy. However, the provision of services must be upgraded to higher levels. Second, it is important to focus on the quality of the manufacturing industry, especially to improve the intensity of capital and technology, with the strategic goal of integrating high-technology with manufacturing. Third, the promotion of particular enterprises and the diversification of economic development help Hong Kong maintain its leading position in international trade, and as a regional financial centre and cargo centre.

In the readjustment of Hong Kong's economy, it is very important to fully realize the impact of factors from the Mainland. The partnership between Hong Kong and the Mainland provides the strong basis for Hong Kong's economic development and prosperity. It is wise to take advantage of the extensive labor resource, land resources, research and development capacity, and the huge potential consumer market in Mainland China. Combined with Hong Kong's advantages in mobilizing capital, product design, management, the application of technology and distribution, Hong Kong and Mainland China should co-develop by taking full advantage of each other's attributes. Hong Kong and the Mainland must undertake cooperation at a high level and in all directions evolving into close relations and a partnership of mutual economic benefit.

Chapter 2
TAIWAN IN TRANSITION: ADJUSTING TO THE NEW REALITY OF ONE COUNTRY TWO SYSTEMS

Milton D. YEH

Introduction

From 1988 through 1998, cross-Straits transactions reached a level higher than that at any time in the last four decades. Annual trade across the Straits over the last decade was more than US$10 billion, with a US$7 or 8 billion balance in favour of Taiwan. With such huge benefits from cross-Straits trade, why are the Taiwan authorities still taking a go-slow approach to promoting trade and investment in China? If China needs capital and management skills from Taiwanese businessmen, then what was the motivation for Beijing to conduct missile tests in the waters near Taiwan in the second half of 1995?

While some China watchers described Taiwan as the trouble maker, others blamed China. In fact, neither perspective provides an adequate explanation. It is this author's view that the internal political structure of Beijing and Taipei largely determines the actions of China and Taiwan. Reference to the internal political structure is used to conceptualize its impact on policy goals, the decision making processes, and the dynamics of political forces of the respective regimes.[1] To understand the pattern of cross-Straits relations, one must examine the dynamics of the internal political structures of both regimes. As such, this chapter does not specifically address Hong Kong's transition to China *per se*. Rather, the notion of "one China," as it arises from the "one country two systems" formula for Hong Kong, serves as the starting point for the following analysis. This chapter argues that potential conflicts across the Taiwan Straits stem from different perceptions of the one China principle endorsed by Beijing and Taipei. This chapter will address three questions. First, what are the underlying political motives of Beijing and Taipei when they advocate the one China principle? Second, in order to meet domestic political needs, how do both regimes reinforce the principle of one China? Third, how do Beijing and Taipei apply the principle of one China to the cross-Straits relationship?

Origin of the One China Debate: Sharing Legitimacy and Confrontation — 1940s–1970s

If one presumes that China and Taiwan remain a whole country, cross-Straits relations are apparently a continuation of the Chinese Civil War which began in the late 1920s. After the fall of Qing Dynasty in 1911, both the Kuomintang (KMT) and the Chinese Communist Party (CCP) have never ceased competing with each other for the legitimate rule in the Chinese community, including Mainland China, Taiwan and the community of overseas Chinese.

---

[1] The analysis is principally based on the argument of Kenneth N. Waltz, see Kenneth N. Waltz, *Man, the State and War: A Theoretical Analysis*, New York: Columbia University Press, 1959, Chapter IV, pp. 80–123.

In the period from the 1950s to the 1970s, both Taiwan and China expressed the principle of one China to legitimatize their rule over the whole of China. While Beijing labeled Taipei a puppet of American imperialism, Taipei reviled the CCP as a traitor to China. Both the KMT and the CCP claimed their respective regimes as the sole legal government of China and the repository of Chinese sovereignty. While the KMT regime insisted that the Chinese mainland was a part of the territory of the government of the Republic of China (ROC), the CCP maintained that Taiwan was an inalienable part of Chinese territory. Does the one China theory matter to the legitimacy of both the KMT and the CCP? It does indeed.

For Taiwan, from 1950 to 1990, there were no national elections to serve as the basis for ROC government rule. The legitimacy of the ruling KMT had been rooted in the concept of one China. According to the one China principle outlined above, the ROC government declared that it had sovereignty over Mainland China and defined the CCP as a rebel group. Under the one China principle, three former presidents — Chiang Kai-shek, Yen Chia-kan, and Chiang Ching-kuo — implemented martial law and the "Temporary Provisions Effective During the Period of the Suppression of the Communist Rebellion," while the ROC Constitution from Mainland China was temporarily frozen. In the last four decades, Taipei's version of one China indeed played a part in its claim for legitimacy.

For Beijing, too, the one China policy has been an effective instrument for the CCP in maintaining its legitimate rule over all of China. The phrase, one China, meant a unified China. Symbolically, the expression of one China connotes the CCP's irreplaceable leading role in spite of the totalitarian nature of its regime. In a geographical sense, the character of one China implies the integrity of the Chinese territory, despite the fact that for whatever reason and methods, the CCP has "occupied" the territory of the Chinese mainland since the Civil War in the 1940s. Under the cover of pursuing a one China policy, the CCP agitated nationalistic sentiments whenever it felt they were needed. The one China policy also provided a sound basis for the CCP to coercively suppress dissident activities in general and minority ethnic unrest in particular. No single political figure in China would dare to risk his political career by proposing even the slightest change in this one China position.

One China versus "One China, Two Political Entities": Legitimacy Needs Still Prevail

Entering into the period of opening up to the world economic system since the late 1970s, Beijing still needs to maintain the one China principle to modify its hard authoritarian rule over the whole of China. The CCP revolutionary regime remains concerned about the integrity of Chinese territory, often reminding themselves of the bitter experience of humiliation by the imperialist powers. The one China argument also provides Beijing a convenient nationalistic rationale for its dealings with Taiwan, the handover of Hong Kong, and also in justifying its attitude to the issue of Tibet, ethnic unrest in Xinjiang Province or other potential minority clashes in the future. Regardless of whether it is right or wrong, the one China appeal has helped the CCP leadership solicit enough political support among the Han people — the predominant ethnic group in China. The symbolism of one China has also been useful for the CCP in promoting the integrity of Chinese society, particularly when divergent interests and conflicts arose among different social sectors mushroomed after the implementation of economic reform since the late 1970s. From this viewpoint, it is not surprising that the incumbent CCP government still maintains its traditional version of the one China vision. While the Chinese Communists stuck to the classical version of one China to maintain their legitimacy on the Mainland, the KMT introduced democracy as an alternative option for maintaining its legitimacy on the island of Taiwan. Different versions of one China are now being aired by different political forces in Taiwan.

From the 1950s to the 1980s, Communist Chinese military actions against Taiwan, combined with Beijing's persistence in maintaining a static notion of one China, made the KMT's authoritarian rule under martial law in Taiwan seem rational. The miraculous economic progress that took off in the 1970s further enhanced the Taiwanese people's recognition and acceptance of KMT rule. However, since the 1980s an increasingly indigenous political elite, which emerged via Taiwan's regular open elections, began to question and challenge the KMT's legitimacy. The implementation of economic reform and opening-up policies in China also meant that the KMT on Taiwan could no longer ensure popular support only by achieving economic progress and exaggerating the danger of Chinese Communism. Thus, it had to re-establish its legitimacy by winning in competitive elections. In the late 1980s, therefore, political reform became necessary in Taiwan.

Democratization in Taiwan began during the tenure of former President Chiang Ching-kuo. In 1987, he made the announcement lifting martial law. This action paved the way for Taiwan to embark on liberalization and democratization. In January 1988, Taiwan deregulated registration procedures for newspapers and removed limits on the number of pages a newspaper could publish per day. Deregulation of television media soon followed. These measures guaranteed the fulfillment of freedom of expression. In February 1989, Taiwan's government modified codes in the Civic Organization Law permitting Taiwanese citizens to organize political parties. These liberalization measures gave Taiwanese people the right to exercise a true democracy. Following these liberalization measures, the current President Lee Teng-hui focused his efforts primarily on the task of democratization.

To lay the legal groundwork for Taiwan's democratization, Lee Teng-hui as President, and as Chairman of the KMT, undertook revisions to the ROC Constitution which was originally drafted in 1945 with the involvement of the CCP. In order to achieve this, President Lee made two quasi-constitutional claims to override the original Constitution and to lay a legal groundwork for direct elections by Taiwanese citizens only. These two quasi-constitutional moves signaled a shift in Taiwan's policy towards the Chinese mainland. In 1990, when Lee Teng-hui was sworn in as the eighth president of the ROC, he announced the suspension of the "period of suppression of the Chinese communist rebellion." Two years later, in 1992, he announced a policy of "one China, two political entities." The policy of one China, two political entities emphasized three points including: 1) "One China" means the ROC, which was founded in 1912 and whose sovereignty covers all of China; 2) The ROC's current jurisdiction covers Taiwan, Penghu, Quemoy and Matsu, and; 3) The ROC commits to the realization of a democratic China. Within the quasi-constitutional framework of one China, two political entities, the incumbent KMT on Taiwan can legally override the Constitution which was designed for the whole of China. From this legal basis, the KMT regime on Taiwan initiated measures to restructure Taiwan's legislature and introduced presidential elections to legitimize its rule over the island.

Thus, since the late 1970s China has insisted on retaining the traditional view of one China both to maintain the integrity of its territory and to enhance CCP legitimacy in China. For domestic political needs, however, Taiwan has adopted a "two political entities" view as well as a new version of "one China". Stemming from the need to maintain their political legitimacy, both Beijing and Taipei adhere to their respective versions of the one China principle to debate against each other. The legitimacy question still underlies the political wranglings which characterize cross-Straits relations.

Whereas Taiwan, for domestic political needs, promotes democratization, China advocates the so-called "one country two systems" formula, now implemented in Hong Kong, in pursuit of unification. The competing actions and policies of Beijing and Taipei arise, therefore, as a result of the differing internal political structures of the two regimes.

Beijing's New Unification Drive: A New Version of One China — One Country Two Systems

In May 1978, the PRC revised its Constitution inserting the usual clause calling for the "liberation" of Taiwan. The term "liberation" in this case still implied resorting to the use of military force. By the end of 1978, Deng Xiaoping began advocating a brand new unification plan for Taiwan. Deng Xiaoping proposed three points for the new orientation of Beijing's Taiwan policy. First, the goal would be the unification of China. Second, the reality of Taiwan's current situation would be respected. Third, under the auspices of a local government, Taiwan would be granted sufficient autonomy. Deng elaborated on the first and second points during a meeting with Burmese President U Ne Win on November 14, 1978 in which he stated that Beijing would respect "the reality of Taiwan" in settling the Taiwan issue. He also stated as an example that certain systems in Taiwan and the Taiwan people's lifestyle could remain unchanged.[2] At a meeting with Japanese Prime Minister Masayoshi

---

[2] The Comprehensive Study Group and the Editorial Group of *Dangde wenxian* (Party documents) of the Central Party Literature Research Center, *Sanzhong quanhui yilai de zhongda juece* (Important decisions since the Third Plenary Session [of the CCP's Eleventh Central Committee]), Beijing: Zhongyang wenxian chubanshe, 1994, 312.

Ohira in December 6 1978, Deng further emphasized that Beijing's only condition was that Taiwan must become part of China, and that as a local government of China, Taiwan could have its own military forces and exercise sufficient autonomy.[3]

Stemming from these talks the National People's Congress (NPC) Standing Committee published a "Message to Compatriots in Taiwan" on January 1 1979, to announce the new peaceful unification policy. This was followed immediately by statements from the Standing Committee of the NPC calling for an end to military confrontation between two sides. Around the same time, Beijing's Ministry of Defense announced that it would stop the bombardment of Quemoy. This is the first time since 1949 that Beijing had apparently dispensed with the military presence. On September 30 1981, Ye Jianying further expounded the spirit of Deng Xiaoping's talks in a nine-point proposal which included measures that would show respect for Taiwan's current systems. On January 11 1982, Deng asserted that Ye had, in fact, made a proposal on the practice of two systems in one country. That is, under the premise of a unified China, the socialist and capitalist systems would be maintained on Mainland China and Taiwan respectively.[4] Thus, the "one country two systems" concept took shape.

Since then, peaceful unification according to the one country two systems formula has been the basic principle of Beijing's Taiwan policy. This phrase was aired in the mass media in China. Successive General Secretaries of the Chinese Communist Party, including Hu Yaobang, Zhao Ziyang, and Jiang Zemin, further interpreted this principle and directed CCP and government departments to institute related implementation measures. Prior to examining the different ways Hu, Zhao and Jiang implemented the principle of one country

---

[3] *Ibid.*
[4] *Ibid.*, p. 313.

two systems, it would be useful to discuss the unique processes and patterns of CCP decision-making.

It is clear from the preceding discussion that policy goals of the CCP usually stem from the ideas of its senior cadres. After one or two senior cadres perceive or evaluate the internal and external situations of a particular issue, they usually articulate one simple phrase or several words to capture its essence. In the case of Taiwan, Deng Xiaoping appreciated the unique characteristics of the Taiwan polity enough to propose that unification must respect the "reality" of Taiwan. Based on this premise, Marshall Ye Jianying manufactured the so-called "nine-point proposal" as a set of concrete measures to assure that reality of Taiwan is respected. After Ye's nine-point proposal was circulated and discussed within the Party and then later publicized in the media, the notion of respecting the reality of Taiwan was developed and then embellished by CCP theorists into the big words — "one country two systems". Perceptions of senior CCP cadres not only set the policy goal for this issue, but also framed the scope of a policy within which CCP and governmental officials were to implement specific measures. Following Deng Xiaoping's goal of peaceful unification and the promulgation of the one country two systems formula, three successive General Secretaries introduced measures and regulations to manage cross-Straits relations.

While Hu Yaobang did not make speeches during his tenure that clearly defined Beijing's Taiwan policy, members of his staff published interpretative works on the one country two systems formula. For example, Yan Jiaqi published an article on the meaning and characteristics of the formula.[5] Zhao Ziyang's policy attitude towards Taiwan included "dispelling hostility, seeking consensus,

---

[5] Yan Jiaqi, "The Scientific Meaning and Characteristics of 'One Country, Two Systems'", *Hongqi* (Red Flag), 1985, no. 6, p. 3.

and taking gradual steps to promote reunification." During his tenure from early 1986 to June 1989, when Taiwan started opening up to China, Zhao concentrated on policy implementation and did not alter the principle of the policy established by Deng Xiaoping. Under Zhao's leadership, the Taiwan Affairs Office and research institutions focusing on Taiwanese affairs were re-organized nationwide. Laws and regulations were enacted and implemented to encourage Taiwan businessmen to invest in and trade with Mainland China. Zhao's administration also reinforced measures to promote cooperative endeavours and cultural exchanges.[6]

When Jiang Zemin succeeded Zhao Ziyang after the June 1989 Tiananmen incident, Beijing's Taiwan policy continued to emphasize the principle of peaceful unification according to the one country two systems formula, but with the added condition that Taiwan must become a local government. However, Jiang and other senior cadres have also debated over how to realize the objective — by peaceful methods or by threat of force. From 1989 to 1994, as Jiang Zemin was gradually placing his own loyal staff within the central bureaucracy of the Party, Beijing's Taiwan policy was mainly under the responsibility of Yang Shangkun and Li Peng. Jiang's direct involvement in Taiwan policy began with a speech made on January 30 1995, which contained an eight-point proposal to Taiwan. Faced with accelerated political democratization in Taiwan, Beijing set three short-term objectives. First, to prevent the idea of Taiwan independence from spreading. Second, to promote the establishment of three links (direct trade, mail, and air and shipping services). Third, to advocate political talks. In practice, sharp criticism

---

[6] See Sung Kuo-cheng, "Beijing's Taiwan Policy 1987–91", in *Taihai guanxi baogao 1987-91* (A report on cross-Strait relations 1987–91), Unpublished report of a 1992 research project headed by Director Hih-jaw Lin of the Institute of International Relations, p. 14.

combined with military intimidation have been utilized. Beijing has continued with the use of such combined efforts as appealing to nationalism and economic and trade benefits.

The speedy democratization process in Taiwan since 1990 further led the Beijing authorities to reaffirm its stand on the principle of one China and to strongly oppose the notion of Taiwan independence. Criticizing the idea of Taiwan independence has since emerged as another pillar of Beijing's Taiwan policy.

In 1990, Taiwan was faced with an unstable political situation, including a dispute about revision of the ROC's constitution and rising media pressure to open all parliamentary seats for election. Partly as a result of these political events, the Democratic Progressive Party (DDP) was able to openly express its support for Taiwan independence. Moreover, Taiwan independence advocates residing overseas were invited to participate in a conference on national affairs. Taken together, this led Beijing to believe that the idea of Taiwan independence had begun to spread on Taiwan. As a result, Chinese Premier Li Peng in his government report to the National Peoples' Congress on March 20 1990, warned that some with ulterior motives had whipped up an adverse current agitating for Taiwan independence, thus openly trying to split Taiwan from the motherland. This was the first time Beijing officially asserted its opposition to Taiwan independence.[7] In addition, the ROC government has actively pursued membership for Taiwan in an array of international bodies prompting a very rigid interpretation of one China under the Jiang administration.

To prevent Taiwan's spilt from the motherland, Beijing's Taiwan affairs departments consequently stepped up unification measures, including advocating the establishment of the three links policy, initiating political negotiations, and expanding personnel and other

---

[7] *Guangming ribao* (Guangming Daily), 22 March 1990, p. 2.

exchanges.[8] More recently, with the exception of a temporary cooling down of cross-Strait relations arising from the Qiandao Lake tragedy (the murder of a group Taiwan tourists in Zhejiang province), the Jiang administration has continued to promote cross-Strait relations according to a combination of the one China and one country two systems premises.

Following the April 1993 meeting between Koo Chen-fu of the Straits Exchanges Foundation (SEF) and Wang Daohan of the Association for Relations Across the Taiwan Straits (ARATS) in Singapore, five regular talks on practical issues were held. No concrete agreement was reached, but a foundation for future cross-Strait political talks was laid. Moreover, in Jiang's eight-point statement of January 30 1995, he proposed holding talks on a cease-fire agreement. Such a proposal, under the one China principle and one country two systems formula, was a new attempt by Jiang Zemin to implement Beijing's policy to engage Taiwan in political talks.

Jiang's proposal did not gain an immediate concrete response, for in 1995 the KMT regime on Taiwan was again in the midst of an intra-party power struggle. On the other hand, ROC President Lee Teng-hui's visit to the United States for a speech at his alma mater, Cornell University, gave Beijing's leftists an excuse for action. To prevent the diplomatic effect of Lee's visit from expanding, Beijing opted for sharp criticisms coupled with military intimidation towards Taiwan. Jiang Zemin's desire to emphasize talks did not ward off the leftists' advocacy of severe measures toward Taiwan.

In fact, the Jiang administration's Taiwan policy has frequently faced similar challenges. Wang Daohan has, for example, interpreted

---

[8] For instance, the contents of the resolution adopted by the National conference on the Work toward Taiwan held on December 6–13, 1990, in Beijing. See *Renmin ribao* (People's Daily) (Beijing), 13 December 1990, p. 1.

Jiang's eight-point proposal as Beijing's present general strategy for solving the Taiwan problem through "promoting peaceful unification, stable development, unity and cooperation, and a prosperous Chinese state."[9] However, in contrast to Wang's low profile remarks on peace, Qiao Shi, then Chairman of the NPC Standing Committee, not only repeatedly claimed Beijing's firm opposition to Taiwan's independence,[10] but also pointed out that for as long as Taiwan does not return to the embrace of the motherland, the United States will have the upper hand in Beijing-Washington relations.[11] Qiao's view of the Taiwan issue as the biggest obstacle to Beijing-Washington relations indicates his intention to adopt severe measures in suppressing Taiwan independence tendencies and solving the Taiwan issue by diplomatic maneuvering.

Deng Xiaoping's one country two systems formula under the principle of one China has always been the core of the Taiwan policy of the Hu, Zhao, and Jiang administrations, though implementation measures adopted by each leader have been different. While the measures they have undertaken were in response to Taiwan's political changes, the respective methods of implementation have been the reflection of CCP intra-party debates.

Taiwan's Mainland Policy: Inter-Party Debates

On 2 November 1987, the then President of Taiwan, Chiang Ching-kuo, announced that mainlanders who had come over with the KMT around 1949 — mostly retired servicemen — would be allowed to visit their families on the mainland. This announcement,

---

[9] *Lianhe bao* (United Daily News) (Taipei), 21 February 1995, p. 4.
[10] For instance, Qiao Shi's talks in Tokyo. See *Zhongguo shibao* (China Times) (Taipei), 14 April 1995, p. 2.
[11] *South China Morning Post*, 20 February 1995, p. 7.

though a very cautious step, marked a big shift in Taipei's policy toward its counterpart and has had a lasting impact on the pattern of relations between the two sides. In 1987 Chiang Ching-kuo also made an announcement lifting martial law. This action paved the way for Taiwan to embark on the path of liberalization and democratization. As a result, in Taiwan today, ideologies of different political forces and public opinion can be freely transmitted and have begun to play a role in the governmental decision-making process. Taiwan's Mainland policy is no exception.

As indicated above, the incumbent KMT leadership started reforming the polity of Taiwan in the early 1990s. Before that period, the main opposition party, the Democratic Progressive Party (DDP) promoted the idea of Taiwan independence to challenge the KMT's principle of one China. With the goal of Taiwan independence, the DDP has successfully mobilized the indigenous Taiwanese political elite as activists for the party. The ideology of Taiwan independence indeed help the DDP to become a strong political force on Taiwan.

In order to reduce the appeal of the principle of Taiwan independence among the in Taiwanese electorate, the incumbent KMT leadership created a "one China, two political entities" proposal in which the two political entities position was in essence similar to the Taiwan independence argument. However, this move by the KMT forced some of its disaffected followers to create another opposition party — the New Party (NP). Immediately after the KMT proposed the one China, two political entities principle, the NP became concerned that President Lee Teng-hui's vision was moving away from the goal of unification which the KMT regime had pursued in the previous four decades.

The KMT version of one China, two political entities also caused a split in the DPP. The basic difference between the KMT and the DPP was their respective positions on Mainland policy. Since most

Taiwanese are aware of the Chinese Communists' strong opposition to the idea of Taiwanese independence, most Taiwanese would rather choose the KMT proposal of one China, two political entities than openly support the DPP's pro-independence position. In this context, despite the perceived mismanagement of certain domestic issues in recent years, the KMT still relied on its Mainland policy to remain as the leading political force in Taiwan. To compete with the KMT's rein of power, the current DPP leadership has lowered the tone of its call for Taiwanese independence and proposed a comprehensive engagement with China instead. This move has driven a group of pro-independence activists to leave the DPP. As a result, these previously active members of the DPP established yet another political party — the Nation Building Party. It is clear that in Taiwan today policies towards the Mainland are a central concern for each of the four major political parties.

With reference to public opinion and the electoral process in Taiwan, each of the major political parities will carefully formulate and execute their policies towards Mainland China no matter who is in power.

Conclusion: Does the One China Principle Matter?

We now turn our attention to the future development of the cross-Straits relationship. Does the on-going discussion about the one China principle among the political elite across the Taiwan Straits matter to the prospects of cross-Straits relations? If China fails to address its economic and political problems over the next few years, and if the domestic situation in the Mainland becomes unstable, then the appeal of the one China principle will likely be more strongly endorsed by Chinese leaders regardless of how smoothly cross-Straits relations are managed. Should the hand-over of Hong Kong and Macao proceed successfully over the next five years, unification with Taiwan will emerge as a convenient issue which the Beijing authorities may use to deflect attention away from deep domestic problems in China. Military officers in China may also exaggerate the danger of instability in the Taiwan Straits to pursue inflated requests for budget allocations or special privileges. The more civil officials in China can successfully execute bold economic experiments, the less influence the military may exert in Beijing's decision-making about Taiwan policy. In fact, the one China principle will help the CCP leadership to win the upper hand in cross-Straits relations. Therefore, an optimistic scenario for cross-Straits relations seems probable. Indeed there have been several encouraging developments recently which suggest that relations across the Straits are relatively stable.

First, when applying the one China principle to the relationship across the Straits, Beijing has tacitly consented to the idea of Taiwan presenting its own version. Second, even in the absence of a resumption of formal talks between the Mainland ARATS and the ROC's SEF, both sides initiated direct maritime contact through a transshipment arrangement in April 1997. Subsequently, both sides have also managed to maintain the status of post-handover air and shipping links between Taiwan and Hong Kong. The experience gained from such negotiations between Beijing, Taipei and Hong Kong is encouraging and welcome. Third, ARATS and SEF have recently proposed a resumption in contacts. More importantly, both Taipei and Beijing both seem to recognize the merits of such exchanges between the two societies across the Taiwan Straits.

There seems to be little doubt that as long as the Taipei and Beijing governments maintain effective rule over their divided territories, political legitimacy will force both regimes to express different visions of the one China principle. Moreover, stemming from domestic political needs both Beijing and Taipei will not ignore the symbolic usage of the one China principle. From this perspective, the one China debate across the Taiwan Straits will not be resolved soon. The degree and circumstances by which debate over the one China principle may produce negative "spill back" effects on cross-Straits relations deserves further elaboration. Other encouraging elements of the cross-Straits relationship also deserve more analytical attention. It is hoped that regular contacts between the ARATS and SEF will provide a foundation for Beijing and Taipei to pursue a stable relationship across the Taiwan Straits. Ultimately, from a Taiwanese perspective, the future of cross-Straits relations has less to do with the success or otherwise of one country two systems as it is applied to Hong Kong than with the way in which the one China principle is played out in the domestic politics of China and Taiwan.

Chapter 3
TAIWAN AND THE CHALLENGE OF "SAN TONG" FOR HONG KONG

LUO Qi

Introduction

The retrocession of Hong Kong's sovereignty to China on 1 July 1997 has been widely seen as a crucial juncture for the relationship between mainland China and Taiwan. It was feared that Taiwan might be forced either to resume the "three direct links" with China or to replace Hong Kong with another intermediary.[1] However, more than a year has passed since the handover yet neither the three direct links (hereafter referred as *"san tong"*) have been realized nor has Hong Kong been replaced by any third place. Indeed, both

---

[1] The so-called "three direct links", or *"San Tong"* as termed by the Chinese, refer to direct trade, transport and postal services links across the Taiwan Strait, which have been cut off since the partition of mainland China and Taiwan in 1949. Since the late 1970s, Beijing has been actively promoting the resumption of the direct links between the two sides of the Strait, but Taipei has consistently refused Beijing's request on political and security grounds.

Beijing and Taipei have continued to use Hong Kong as an intermediary to conduct indirect trade in the post-handover period. However, this does not mean that Beijing's tireless campaign for the resumption of *san tong* has lost its momentum. In fact, mainland leaders have kept up their pressure on the Taiwan authorities by renewing their demand for speedy resumption of *san tong* across the Taiwan Strait during the recent high-level talks between Beijing's top negotiator, Mr. Wang Daohan, and his Taiwanese counterpart, Mr. Koo Chen-fu in mainland China (hereafter the Mainland).

Adding to the complexity of this issue are the circumstances of the Asian financial crisis which started in Thailand in July 1997 and which has plunged many countries in Southeast and East Asia, including the Hong Kong Special Administrative Region (SAR), into a deep economic recession. Inevitably, this has had a profound impact on political and economic relations between the three Chinese entities, as well as the performance of their respective economies.

So why have China and Taiwan continued to trade with each other indirectly via Hong Kong since the handover? How has Hong Kong's re-export business performed since its return to China? What effect has the Asian financial crisis had on the trade performance of the three Chinese economies? And, above all, what impact will it have on Hong Kong's re-export trade if one day China and Taiwan decide to resume *san tong* across the Taiwan Strait? This chapter seeks to address each of these questions.

Review of Hong Kong's Trade with China and Taiwan after the Handover

While the Asian financial crisis started in early July 1997, it seemed that its effect on Hong Kong's trade performance did not really set in until early 1998. This can be seen from Table 1, which shows that both Hong Kong's total exports and imports in 1997 achieved a higher growth rate than in 1996. Beginning in early 1998, however, Hong Kong entered an economic downturn as the financial crisis began to affect its economy. Hong Kong's major trading partners in the region, including Japan, South Korea, Taiwan and Singapore, have all been hit to varying degrees by the financial storm, which has led to a severe contraction in Hong Kong's trade with them. As a result, in the first six months of 1998 Hong Kong's domestic exports, re-exports and imports all registered negative growth on a year-on-year basis (by 5.4%, 1.6% and 5.7% respectively).[2] This has had spill-over affects on overall economic performance for the first post-handover year — total trade only managed to expand by 0.8% compared with the previous 12 months (see Table 1).

Performance in the re-exports sector were equally disappointing. The growth rate dropped from 5.4% in the 12 months before the handover to a mere 2.1% in the following 12 months. This is a far cry from the situation in the early 1990s when re-exports grew by nearly 30% per year. However, this setback has not reduced the role of re-exports as the engine of Hong Kong's trade expansion. As is apparent in Table 1, the share of re-exports in total exports has continued to increase in the post-handover period, reaching a staggering 85.7%, largely due to the negative and slower growth of domestic exports and imports. Consequently, the contribution made by re-exports to the growth of Hong Kong's total trade has in fact increased significantly, jumping from 61% to over 108%.[3] This suggests that re-exports will continue as the main driving force

---

[2] Census and Statistics Department, Hong Kong SAR Government: *Press Releases on Statistical Data*, 13 August 1998.

[3] 61% = [5.4% (1,210,080 / 2,988,072)] / 3.6%; 108% = [2.1% (1,235,532 / 3,013,440)] / 0.8%. This latter figure of more than 100% arises because of the negative growth in domestic exports.

TABLE 1: Hong Kong's External Trade, 1991-June 1998

(HK$ million)

	1991	1992	1993	1994	1995	1996	1997	Average annual growth rate (91–97) (%)	July 1996 to June 1997	July 1997 To June 1998	Change in annual growth rate (percentage point)
Domestic exports	231,045 <+2.3>	234,123 <+1.3>	223,027 <-4.7>	222,092 <-0.4>	231,657 <+4.3>	212,160 <-8.4>	211,410 <-0.4>	-1.5	208,764 <-6.3>	206,232 <-1.2>	+5.1
Re-exports	534,841 <+29.2> (69.8)	690,829 <+29.2> (74.7)	823,224 <+19.2> (78.7)	947,921 <+15.1> (81.0)	1,112,470 <+17.4> (82.8)	1,185,758 <+6.6> (84.8)	1,244,539 <+5.0> (85.5)	+15.1	1,210,080 <+5.4> (85.3)	1,235,532 <+2.1> (85.7)	-3.3
Total exports	765,886 <+19.7>	924,953 <+20.8>	1,046,250 <+13.1>	1,170,013 <+11.8>	1,344,127 <+14.9>	1,397,917 <+4.0>	1,455,949 <+4.2>	+11.3	1,418,844 <+3.5>	1,441,764 <+1.6>	-1.9
Imports	778,982 <+21.2>	955,295 <+22.6>	1,072,597 <+12.3>	1,250,709 <+16.6>	1,491,121 <+19.2>	1,535,582 <+3.0>	1,615,090 <+5.2>	+12.9	1,569,228 <+3.7>	1,571,676 <+0.2>	-3.5
Total trade	1,544,868 <+20.5>	1,880,248 <+21.7>	2,118,848 <+12.7>	2,420,722 <+14.2>	2,835,248 <+17.1>	2,933,490 <+3.5>	3,071,040 <+4.7>	+12.1	2,988,072 <+3.6>	3,013,440 <+0.8>	-2.8

Sources: Census and Statistics Department, Hong Kong SAR Government: *Hong Kong External Trade*, various years; *Hong Kong Economic Trend*, August, various years.

Notes: Figures in ( ) refer to percentage shares in Hong Kong's total exports; figures in < > indicate % change over the previous year.

behind Hong Kong's growth in external trade for the foreseeable future.

Table 2 elaborates upon Hong Kong's trade ties with its two major trading partners, China and Taiwan. It demonstrates not only that China-Hong Kong trade has grown much faster than Taiwan-Hong Kong trade, but that it also occupied a far greater share in Hong Kong's total trading activities. For example, in 1997 the volume of China's total trade with Hong Kong was nearly seven times that of Taiwan (HK$1,116 billion vs. HK$161 billion), despite that fact that China's total foreign trade in that year was only 1.4 times that of Taiwan (US$325.2 billion vs. US$236.5 billion). This seems to indicate that China has used Hong Kong as the main gateway to conduct its foreign trade, while Taiwan has relied on other channels to develop its trade with the outside world.

Both China and Taiwan have continued to export and import via Hong Kong after the handover, but at a much slower pace due primarily to weak overall export performances. However, China seemed to have strengthened its position somewhat as Hong Kong's largest supplier of and market for re-exports. This is reflected by the small but steady increase in its shares in Hong Kong's total re-exports by comparison with the 12 months just prior to the handover. Meanwhile, Taiwan supplied fewer re-exports to Hong Kong since the handover, resulting in the first negative growth (−0.7%) in its overall trade with Hong Kong in recent decades.

Table 3 examines the structures of re-exports from China and Taiwan in order to identify the nature and degree of their reliance on Hong Kong's *entrepôt* services. Although China provided nearly 60% of Hong Kong's re-exports, less than 2% of this total actually went to Taiwan. In other words, over 98% of the total was destined for elsewhere in the world. On the other hand, Taiwan contributed less than 7% to Hong Kong's total re-exports, although about 90% of this total was bound for China. Taiwan has apparently utilized

TABLE 2: Hong Kong's Trade with Mainland China and Taiwan, 1991-June 1998

(HK$ million)

	1991	1992	1993	1994	1995	1996	1997	Average annual growth rate (91-97) (%)	July 96 to June 97	July 97 to June 98	% change
Domestic ex. to:											
China	54,404 (23.5)	61,959 (26.5)	63,367 (28.4)	61,009 (27.5)	63,555 (27.4)	61,620 (29.0)	63,867 (30.2)	+2.7	61,836 (29.6) [1](30.6)	63,084 [1](30.6)	+2.0
Taiwan	6,066 (2.6)	6,500 (2.8)	6,261 (2.8)	6,076 (2.7)	7,971 (3.4)	6,705 (3.2)	7,029 (3.3)	+2.5	6,400 (3.1)	7,145 [7](3.5)	+11.6
Re-exports to:											
China	153,318 (28.7)	212,105 (30.7)	274,561 (33.4)	322,835 (34.1)	384,043 (34.5)	417,752 (35.2)	443,878 (35.7)	+19.4	427,896 (35.4)	442,992 [1](35.9)	+3.5
Taiwan	24,765 (4.6)	26,156 (3.8)	21,910 (2.7)	22,416 (2.4)	27,758 (2.5)	26,638 (2.2)	29,582 (2.4)	+3.0	28,044 (2.3)	29,448 [6](2.4)	+5.0
Total exports to:											
China	207,722 (27.1)	274,064 (29.6)	337,928 (32.3)	383,844 (32.8)	447,598 (33.3)	479,372 (34.3)	507,746 (34.9)	+16.1	489,732 (34.5)	506,076 [1](35.1)	+3.3
Taiwan	30,831 (4.0)	32,656 (3.5)	28,171 (2.7)	28,492 (2.4)	35,729 (2.7)	33,344 (2.4)	36,611 (2.5)	+2.9	34,444 (2.4)	36,593 [6](2.5)	+6.2
Imports from:											
China	293,356 (37.6)	354,438 (37.1)	402,161 (37.5)	470,876 (37.6)	539,480 (36.2)	570,443 (37.1)	608,372 (37.7)	+12.9	587,256 (37.4)	605,556 [1](38.5)	+3.1
Taiwan	74,591 (9.6)	87,019 (9.1)	93,968 (8.8)	107,310 (8.6)	129,266 (8.7)	123,202 (8.0)	124,547 (7.7)	+8.9	122,028 (7.8)	118,740 [4](7.6)	-2.7
Re-exports from:											
China	315,689 (59.0)	403,782 (58.4)	474,007 (57.6)	545,831 (57.6)	636,392 (57.2)	683,514 (57.6)	723,416 (58.1)	+14.8	701,340 (58.0)	723,204 [1](58.5)	+3.1
Taiwan	41,693 (7.8)	54,442 (7.9)	64,649 (7.9)	72,060 (7.6)	83,307 (7.5)	82,177 (6.9)	83,341 (6.7)	+12.2	81,516 (6.7)	80,160 [3](6.5)	-1.7
Total trade with											
China	501,078 (32.4)	628,502 (33.4)	740,089 (34.9)	854,720 (35.3)	987,078 (34.8)	1,049,815 (35.8)	1,116,118 (36.3)	+14.3	1,076,988 (36.0)	1,111,632 [1](36.9)	+3.2
Taiwan	105,422 (6.8)	119,675 (6.4)	122,139 (5.8)	135,802 (5.6)	164,995 (5.8)	156,546 (5.3)	161,158 (5.2)	+7.3	156,472 (5.2)	155,333 [4](5.2)	-0.7

Source: As Table1.
Notes: Figures in ( ) refer to percentage shares in Hong Kong's total domestic exports, re-exports, total exports, imports and total trade respectively; figures in [ ] indicate the rank as Hong Kong's trading partner.

TABLE 3: Hong Kong's Re-exports from Mainland China and Taiwan, 1991-June 1998

(HK$ million)

	1991	1992	1993	1994	1995	1996	1997	Average annual growth rate (91-97) (%)	July 1996 to June 1997	July 1997 to June 1998	% change
From China	315,689	403,782	474,007	545,831	636,392	683,514	723,416	+14.8	701,340	723,204	+3.1
Of which: To Taiwan	8,747 (2.8)	8,659 (2.1)	8,538 (1.8)	9,985 (1.8)	12,176 (1.9)	12,249 (1.8)	13,504 (1.9)	+7.5	12,802 (1.8)	13,426 (1.9)	+4.9
To other areas	306,942 (97.2)	395,123 (97.9)	465,469 (98.2)	535,846 (98.2)	624,216 (98.1)	671,265 (98.2)	709,912 (98.1)	+15.0	688,538 (98.2)	709,778 (98.1)	+3.1
From Taiwan	41,693	54,442	64,649	72,060	83,307	82,177	83,341	+12.2	81,516	80,160	-1.7
Of which: To China	36,253 (87.0)	48,657 (89.4)	58,662 (90.7)	65,819 (91.3)	74,455 (89.4)	75,246 (91.6)	75,223 (90.3)	+12.9	74,335 (91.2)	72,058 (89.9)	-3.1
To other areas	5,440 (13.0)	5,785 (10.6)	5,987 (9.3)	6,241 (8.7)	8,852 (10.6)	6,931 (8.4)	8,118 (9.7)	+6.9	7,181 (8.8)	8,102 (10.1)	+12.8

Sources: Table 2; Board of Foreign Trade, Ministry of Economic Affairs, ROC Government; *Zhonggong duiwai jingmao yanjiu* (Studies on Communist China's Foreign Economic and Trade Activities), various issues.

Note: Figures in ( ) refer to percentage shares in Hong Kong's re-exports originated from China and Taiwan respectively.

Hong Kong as the main conduit for its indirect trade with China, whereas China has used Hong Kong mainly to channel its exports to other parts of the world.

Table 4 illustrates the same phenomenon from the opposite perspective. China was the destination for over 35% of Hong Kong's total re-exports, but only about 17% of this total actually originated in Taiwan. Thus, the overwhelming majority of re-exports into China via Hong Kong originated from elsewhere in the world. On the other hand, Taiwan received less than 2½% of the total re-exports from Hong Kong, although nearly 46% of that was China-sourced. On the whole, re-exports from China to Taiwan in the first 12 months after the handover increased by nearly 5% over the previous 12 months, while the opposite flow shrank by over 3%.

This analysis suggests that the re-export business in Hong Kong has played a crucial role in stimulating the growth of its external trade, and that China and Taiwan, for various reasons and to varying degrees have over the years contributed to the rapid expansion of re-export activities by conducting their indirect trade via Hong Kong. Hong Kong as an *entrepôt* centre is more important to China than to Taiwan in developing their trade with foreign countries, but becomes more significant to Taiwan relative to China in conducting indirect trade with one another.

Why have China and Taiwan continued to utilize Hong Kong to conduct their indirect trade after Hong Kong was returned to China? From an economic point of view two factors seem to be prominent. First, there is no seaport currently in China and Taiwan that can match the handling capacity and efficiency provided by Hong Kong which has consistently been ranked at the top of the world's Port Traffic League in terms of container throughput in recent years.[4]

---

[4] See Mark Lambert (ed.) *Containerisation International Yearbook 1998* (London: EMAP Business Communications Ltd, March 1997), pp. 8–9.

TABLE 4: Hong Kong's Re-exports to Mainland China and Taiwan, 1991-June 1998

(HK$ million)

	1991	1992	1993	1994	1995	1996	1997	Average annual growth rate (91-97) (%)	July 1996 to June 1997	July 1997 to June 1998	% ch
To China	153,318	212,105	274,561	322,835	384,043	417,752	443,878	+19.4	427,896	442,992	+:
Of which:											
From Taiwan	36,253 (23.6)	48,657 (22.9)	58,662 (21.4)	65,819 (20.4)	76,455 (19.9)	75,246 (18.0)	75,223 (16.9)	+12.9	74,335 (17.4)	72,058 (16.3)	-:
From other areas	117,065 (76.4)	163,448 (77.1)	215,899 (78.6)	257,016 (79.6)	307,588 (80.1)	342,506 (82.0)	368,655 (83.1)	+21.1	353,561 (82.6)	370,934 (83.7)	+:
To Taiwan	24,765	26,156	21,910	22,416	27,758	26,638	29,582	+3.0	28,044	29,448	+:
Of which:											
From China	8,747 (35.3)	8,659 (33.1)	8,538 (39.0)	9,985 (44.5)	12,176 (43.9)	12,249 (46.0)	13,504 (45.6)	+7.5	12,802 (45.6)	13,426 (45.6)	+:
From other areas	16,018 (64.7)	17,497 (66.9)	13,372 (61.0)	12,431 (55.5)	15,582 (56.1)	14,389 (54.0)	16,078 (54.4)	+0.1	15,242 (54.4)	16,022 (54.4)	+:

Source: As Table 3.
Note: Figures in ( ) refer to percentage shares in Hong Kong's re-exports destined for China and Taiwan respectively.

Although Taiwan has two good ports, Kaohsiung and Keelung, ranking third and eleventh place respectively in the League in 1996, an estimated 50% of Taiwan's total foreign trade cargo (over 9 million TEUs in 1996) was transferred via Hong Kong. Not surprisingly, nearly 30% of all container ships sailing through Taiwan's ports (about 60,000 vessel/times in 1996), be they local or foreign, ply the Taiwan-Hong Kong route.[5] China, on the other hand, lags far behind Hong Kong and Taiwan in the development of port facilities. At the moment, none of its ports is able to accommodate fourth- or fifth-generation container ships (with a capacity of 3,000 TEUs or above) and a large part of its exports and imports has to be carried by feeders to and from Hong Kong. It is believed that this situation will likely remain unchanged for at least another 5–7 years.[6] Hong Kong will thus continue as the most important intermediary for maritime trade between Taiwan and China in the short to medium term.

Second, through re-exporting activities via Hong Kong both China and Hong Kong have incurred a handsome trade surplus. As can be seen from Table 2, in the first 12 months after the handover China registered a surplus of HK$280,212 million from its re-export trade with Hong Kong. This was 2.8 times the overall surplus for its total trade with Hong Kong (HK$99,480 million). During the same period, Taiwan recorded a surplus of HK$50,712 million from its re-export trade with Hong Kong, contributing 62% to its overall surplus for total trade with Hong Kong (HK$82,147 million). Obviously, this provided a strong financial incentive for both China

---

[5] Ling Yun, "The oriental pearl is still shining: assessing Hong Kong's position as a shipping centre after the 1997-handover", *Touzi Zhongguo* (Investing in China), Taipei, July 1997, p. 56.
[6] Li Er, "On problems in cross-Strait transportation", *Jingji qianzhan* (Economic Outlook), Taipei, July 5, 1997, p. 41.

and Taiwan to continue utilizing Hong Kong's re-exporting services in the post-handover period.

The Impact of Re-exports between China and Taiwan

Prior to the handover, it was feared that re-exports between China and Taiwan via Hong Kong would decrease after the handover. Some of this concern arose as a result of on-going efforts by the business communities on both sides of the Taiwan Strait to shift their indirect trade from an onshore to an offshore operation, and Taiwan's attempt to replace Hong Kong with other intermediaries such as the Ishigaki Island in Japan and Pusan in South Korea.[7] Indeed, the first 12 months after the handover saw a 3.1% drop in re-exports from Taiwan to China, the biggest fall since the two sides resumed large-scale economic contacts ten years ago (see Tables 3 and 4). Does this signal the beginning of the end of Hong Kong's unique role as an intermediary for the re-export business between China and Taiwan?

It is imperative at this point to determine whether or not the handover of Hong Kong in July 1997 has accelerated the decline in re-exports between China and Taiwan via Hong Kong. As shown in

---

[7] There was an intensive debate on this issue in Taiwan, as cited in Tien Hung-mao, "Is Hong Kong vital to the PRC wooing of Taiwan?", in Wang Gungwu and Wong Siu-lun (eds.), *Hong Kong in the Asia-Pacific Region: Rising to the New Challenges* (Hong Kong: Centre of Asian Studies, University of Hong Kong, 1997), pp. 48–49. For scholarly discussions on this issue, also see Yan Zhong-da, "Studies on changes in Hong Kong's intermediary role after the 97-Handover", Chung Hwa Institute for Economic Research (ed.), *Liangan jingji qingxin fenxi* (Analyses on Cross-Strait Economic Situations, 1995/96), a report commissioned by Mainland Affairs Council, ROC Government, Taipei, June 1997, pp. 235-61; Huang Hui-feng, "Taiwan's new role after the 97-Handover in Hong Kong", *Touzi Zhongguo*, August, 1997, pp. 78–83.

Table 5, re-exports between China and Taiwan have started a relative decline since 1990, almost stagnating in absolute terms between 1995 and 1997. This was mainly due to the increased efforts to shift from onshore trade (re-exports) to offshore trade (transshipment, transit and even direct trade) by both Mainland and Taiwanese traders and shipping companies.[8] As a result, the total trade between China and Taiwan (including re-exports via Hong Kong) has expanded much faster than re-exports, as indicated by the wide gap of 8.7 percentage points between the two average growth rates for the period of 1994 and 1997. This caused the share of re-exports in total China-Taiwan trade to drop steadily, from over 80% in 1990 to 49% just 12 months before the handover (see Table 5). Thus, it seems reasonable to expect this trend of decline to continue during the post-handover period.

A further point to bear in mind when analyzing the trends in re-exports between China and Taiwan in the post-handover period is the profound impact of the on-going Asian financial crisis. Hong Kong's first post-handover year coincided with the beginning of the Asian financial crisis which has thrown many countries in Southeast and East Asia into economic turmoil. The three Chinese economies have, to varying degrees, also been affected, with their external trade sectors among the first to fall victim to the crisis. For example, in the first six months of 1998 Hong Kong's total exports fell by 2.1% over the same period of 1997 while Taiwan's fell by 7.1%. China, though somewhat less affected by the crisis, still witnessed a

---

[8] For more detailed studies on the forms of cross-Strait trade, see Sung Yun-wing, "'Direct trade' between the two sides of the Taiwan Strait", in Liao Kwan-sheng (ed.) *Liangan jingmao hudong de yinyou yu shengji* (Dynamics and Problems in the Economic Interaction between China and Taiwan) (Taipei: Yongchen Wenhua Publishing House, 1995), pp. 35–47; K. C. Fung, *Trade and Investment: Mainland China, Hong Kong and Taiwan* (Hong Kong: City University of Hong Kong Press, 1997), Chapter 3.

TABLE 5: Trade between Taiwan and Mainland China, 1990 - June 1998

(US$ million)

	Total Taiwan trade with China		Taiwan exports to China		Taiwan imports from China		Trade balance	
	Re-exports via HK	Total trade	Re-exports via HK	Total exports	Re-exports via HK	Total imports	Re-exports via HK	Total balance
1990	4,044 (81.9)	4,937	3,278 (78.6)	4,171	765	-----	2,513 (73.8)	3,406
1991	5,793 (71.9)	8,054	4,667 (67.4)	6,928	1,126	-----	3,451 (59.5)	5,802
1992	7,407 (68.5)	10,816	6,288 (64.8)	9,697	1,119	-----	5,169 (60.3)	8,578
1993	8,689 (62.8)	13,832	7,585 (59.6)	12,728	1,104	-----	6,482 (55.8)	11,615
1994	9,810 (59.4)	16,512	8,517 (58.1)	14,653	1,292 (69.5)	1,859	7,225 (56.5)	12,794
1995	11,457 (54.6)	20,990	9,883 (55.2)	17,898	1,574 (50.9)	3,091	8,309 (56.1)	14,807
1996	11,300 (50.9)	22,208	9,718 (50.8)	19,148	1,582 (51.7)	3,060	8,135 (50.6)	16,089
1997	11,459 (46.9)	24,440	9,715 (47.3)	20,525	1,744 (44.6)	3,915	7,971 (48.0)	16,610
Average annual growth rate (%) (94-97)	+5.3	+14.0	+4.5	+11.9	+10.5	+28.2	+3.3	+9.1
July 96 To June 97	11,253 (48.7)	23,100	9,600 (48.7)	19,700	1,653 (48.6)	3,400	7,947 (48.7)	16,300
July 96 To June 98	11,040 (45.5)	24,251	9,306 (46.4)	20,062	1,734 (41.4)	4,189	7,572 (47.7)	15,873
% change	-1.9	+4.9	-3.1	+1.8	+4.9	+23.2	-4.7	-2.7

Source: Board of Foreign Trade, Ministry of Economic Affairs, ROC Government: *Zhonggong duiwai jingmao yanjiu* (Studies on Communist China's Foreign Economic and Trade Activities), various issues.

Notes: ----- mean data not available; figures in ( ) refer to percentage shares of re-exports via HK in total trade, exports, imports and trade balance between Taiwan and mainland respectively.

sharp slowdown in its export growth, dropping to only 7.6% compared with the 21% growth it had achieved for all of 1997.[9] Clearly, this put more downward pressure on re-exports between China and Taiwan for the 1997–1998 period. For example, Taiwan has already attributed the 3.1% fall in re-exports from Taiwan to China (via Hong Kong) in the first post-handover year to sluggish market demand and weak export performance on the part of China.[10]

Despite this difficult international economic environment, the percentage share of re-exports between China and Taiwan in Taiwan's total exports remained steady at 7.9%, a 0.2 percentage point drop compared with that for the previous 12 months. However, between 1994 and 1997 the share dropped from 9.15 to 7.96%, decreasing by 0.4 percentage point per year.[11] This means that the decline in re-exports from Taiwan to China (via Hong Kong) in the first post-handover year has actually slowed, contrary to the expectation that the downward trend would be accelerated after the handover. Meanwhile, re-exports from China to Taiwan (via Hong Kong) in the first post-handover year have continued to grow, by 4.9% compared with the previous 12 months (see Tables 3 and 4).

Thus, there is no sign to indicate that the handover of Hong Kong in July 1997 has accelerated the decline in re-exports between China and Taiwan. Nor is there any evidence to suggest that the 3.1% drop in re-exports from Taiwan to China (via Hong Kong) in

---

[9] Census and Statistics Department, Hong Kong SAR Government, *Press Release*; Board of Foreign Trade, Ministry of Economic Affairs, ROC Government, *Guoji maoyi qingshi fenxi* (An Analysis of International Trade), 20 July 1998; *Liangan jingmao tongxun* (The Information of Cross-Strait Trade), Taipei, 10 September 1998.

[10] Board of Foreign Trade, Ministry of Economic Affairs, ROC Government, *Guoji maoyi*, p. 1.

[11] Based on the figures provided in Board of Foreign Trade, Ministry of Economic Affairs, ROC Government, *Zhonggong duiwai jingmao yanjiu* (Studies on Communist China's Foreign Trade), Taipei, Issue 509, 16 June 1998, pp. 16, 19.

the first year after the handover was caused more by the post-handover effect than by the impact of the financial crisis. For now at least, both China and Taiwan appear to have no intention to reduce the use of Hong Kong to channel trade with each other. That is to say, they are still quite dependent on the re-export services provided by Hong Kong, though for differing political and economic reasons.

The importance of re-exports between China and Taiwan to Hong Kong's total re-export business must now be examined. Table 6 shows that China-Taiwan re-exports only accounted for a small and still decreasing share in Hong Kong's total re-exports — merely 7.1% in 1997 — and contributed only about 0.1 to 2 percentage points to the growth of total re-exports (+5%). This means that the growth of total re-exports in Hong Kong today is almost entirely sustained by the rapid expansion of other re-exports, hence the impact of losing re-exports between China and Taiwan on the total re-export business would be quite limited should China and Taiwan decide to trade with each other directly.[12]

However, the question remains, would Hong Kong lose all the re-export business if *san tong* between China and Taiwan becomes a reality? The answer seems to be no. The first reason is that those re-exports originating from and destined for Guangdong Province and adjacent areas, where a large number of export-oriented foreign-funded firms operate, will still have to be channeled though Hong Kong. Furthermore, the newly built Beijing-Kowloon railway has

---

[12] For more detailed discussions on the impact of the resumption of direct trading between China and Taiwan on Hong Kong external trade, see Sung Yun-wing, "'Direct trade' between the two sides", in Liao Kwan-sheng (ed.); Kao Chang and Sung Yun-wing, *Liangan sandi jianjie maoyi de shizheng fenxi* (Empirical Study on the Indirect Trade between China, Hong Kong and Taiwan), a report commissioned by the Mainland Affairs Council, ROC Government, Taipei, September 1995, Chapter 7.

greatly widened Hong Kong's economic hinterland in China which will certainly attract more business to Hong Kong's re-export trade.[13]

Secondly, it is believed that Hong Kong's superiority in providing efficient and effective customs, port, legal, financial, insurance, consulting and information services, and especially in connecting businesses between China and Taiwan and between Chinese and foreign interests, will continue to attract both Chinese and foreign businesses to Hong Kong's re-export services. Thus, it seems certain that a considerable proportion of the current re-export activities between China and Taiwan would be retained by Hong Kong if China and Taiwan start to deal with each other directly.

Impact of an Offshore Transshipment Centre

While the preceding section addressed re-exports between China and Taiwan, it is also necessary to recognize that not all re-exports from China or Taiwan go to the other side of the Strait. As illustrated in Tables 2 and 3, China, as the single largest supplier, has over the years provided nearly 60% of Hong Kong's total re-exports in contrast to barely 7% from Taiwan. Of those goods from China, as much as 98% were actually bound for third places (i.e. foreign countries), with the remaining 2% for Taiwan. On the other hand, Tables 2 and 4 demonstrate that China, again as the largest market destination, has absorbed about 35% of Hong Kong's total re-exports, as opposed to just 2½% by Taiwan. Of those goods shipped to China, over 80% came from foreign countries, with the other 20% from Taiwan. More importantly, re-exports between China and foreign countries has grown much faster than those between China and Taiwan, as indicated by the huge gaps of

---

[13] One estimation puts this proportion around 50%. See *Liangan jingmao tongxun*, 10 November 1997, p. 18.

average growth rates in Tables 3 and 4. That is, re-exports between China and foreign countries, not those between China and Taiwan, have been the main driving force behind the rapid growth of Hong Kong's re-export trade in recent years. Therefore, any attempt to divert this part of the re-export business away from Hong Kong would have a more significant impact on its re-export business.

Just such a threat has emerged since April 1997 with a new shipping route carrying China's exports to and imports from foreign countries being added into cross-Strait trade, namely, the "Offshore Transshipment Centre" as it is known in Taiwan, or "Fixed-point Direct Shipping" as China refers to it. Following long and arduous negotiations and related preparations, Beijing and Taipei approved applications from six Taiwanese shipping companies and six from China to use their foreign-registered vessels to operate a direct cargo shipping service between Fuzhou and Xiamen on the Mainland and Kaohsiung in Taiwan. This was the first, officially approved direct shipping link between the two sides of the Taiwan Strait since 1949, despite the fact that the two sides have technically not formally ended a state of war with each other. The beginning of this historic operation was marked by the arrival of a vessel belonging to the Xiamen Shipping Corporation (registered in St. Vincent) at the Kaohsiung Port on 19 April 1997. This new operation could divert part of the re-export trade between China and foreign countries away from Hong Kong, increasing the pressure on Hong Kong's struggle to maintain its position as one of the world's leading *entrepôt* centres. But how effective has this operation been so far? Is it really a threat to Hong Kong's re-export trade?

According to official records, by the end of March of 1998 a total of ten vessels (six from China and four from Taiwan) had participated in this operation, with an average handling capacity of 397 TEUs per vessel. Together they had made a total of 1,286 voyages between the two sides of the Strait and carried about

165,000 TEUs of cargo.[14] That is to say, on average each vessel only carried 128.3 TEUs per voyage, a mere 32% of the average capacity of each vessel. One survey found that some vessels travelled without any cargo on board or sometimes with empty containers.[15] Only ten vessels from the 12 companies had been involved, meaning that at least two companies had not started their operations almost a year after the commencement of the direct shipping link. Indeed, the three approved Taiwanese companies (Wanhai, Nantai and Jianheng), after having fought very hard to get the operating licence, hesitated for at least two months before starting their operations.[16] After a few months into the operation, all the companies involved but one had reportedly incurred an operational loss, although the situation seemed to improve marginally in the ensuing months.[17]

The fundamental reason for the extensive losses was that there was not a sufficient amount of cargo available for the vessels to carry. This can be attributed to two factors. The first, has to do with the rules governing the operation of the Offshore Transhipment Centre. Based on the grand principle of no direct trading across the Strait, the Taiwan authorities only permitted foreign-registered vessels to carry mainland cargo bound for a third place (e.g. in Europe or North American) and foreign goods for the Mainland could only be brought to the Transhipment Centre in Kaohsiung for re-export. As such, these goods were not permitted to pass through Taiwanese customs or to enter Taiwan's internal markets. A brief stoppage at

---

[14] *Wen Hui Pao* (Wen Hui Daily), Hong Kong, 16 April 1998, p. A5.
[15] Gong Chun-sheng, "On cross-Strait business opportunities and the Offshore Transhipment Centre", *Zhonggong dalu yanjiu* (Studies on Mainland China), Taipei, No. 9, 1997, p. 41.
[16] Lin Li, "What is the economic basis for the Offshore Transhipment Operation?", *Touzi Zhongguo*, June 1997, p. 44.
[17] Ling Yun, "Is 97 An Opportunity or Crisis for Hong Kong?", *Touzi Zhongguo*, August 1997, p. 48; *Wen Hui Pao*, 16 April 1998, p. A5.

the Centre for simple processing or re-packaging was, however, permitted. These restrictions, of course, drastically reduced the volume of cargo eligible for such shipment.

The second reason relates to the limitations of the Mainland ports selected. Fuzhou and Xiamen are small ports in China, handling only 31 million tons of cargo between them, or 3.4% of the national total in 1997.[18] In terms of container throughput, roughly 500,000 TEUs currently pass through the two ports each year, but only about 3000 TEUs were destined for foreign countries each month.[19] So if all ten vessels travelled once a week, on average each vessel could only carry about 75 TEUs on each voyage.

Thus, despite its symbolic importance, the so-called Offshore Transshipment Centre or Fixed-Point Direct Shipping is economically unsustainable in the long run. It appears that China and Taiwan launched the operation largely on the basis of political considerations. From Beijing's point of view, although a partial direct link was not really what it was after, it is nevertheless an important step forward to the eventual resumption of *san tong*. Taipei, on the other hand, sees the operation as a crucial step to revitalize its ambitious Asia Pacific Operation Centres Plan, which has made little substantive progress since it was launched in 1995 owing primarily to the poor political relationship with Beijing.[20] The shipping link was also used to help ease the pressure on the Taiwan government brought about by both local and foreign businesses which have been critical of its Mainland economic policies. It therefore seems

---

[18] State Statistical Bureau, PRC Government, *Zhongguo tongji zhaiyao* (A Statistical Survey of China, 1998) (Beijing: China Statistical Publishing House, 1998), p. 124.
[19] Li Guang-xu *et al.*, "On the prospects of Offshore Transhipment Operation", *Touzi Zhongguo*, March 1997, pp. 23–26.
[20] The Plan aims to build Taiwan into manufacturing, finance, maritime transport, air transport, telecommunication and media hubs by the early 21st Century.

that both Beijing and Taipei were prepared to forgo some economic interests in the short term in order to achieve political goals in the long term.

There are perhaps two ways to solve the loss-making problem. First, Taipei could remove the "no customs clearance, no entry to the domestic market" restriction so as to allow vessels to carry cargo bound for each other's domestic markets. However, this would be tantamount to direct trading with China which is still strictly forbidden by the Taiwanese government in accordance with its *National Unification Guidelines* and so remains as an unlikely scenario. Second, Beijing could open its major international ports, such as Dalian, Tianjin, Qinghuangdao, Ningbo and Shanghai to this operation as well in order to increase the supply of cargo to those vessels able to use the Transshipment Centre. Together, the five ports handled nearly 463 million tons of cargo, more than half of China's total in 1997,[21] and provided staple business for China's mostly under-utilized, state-owned maritime freight carriers. Unless a major breakthrough emerges in connection with the *san tong* issue to justify a radical internal restructuring among the carriers, China is unlikely at this stage to open all these big ports and grant exclusive rights to a small number of companies to run a lucrative business while allowing the majority to go "starving".

As far as the impact on Hong Kong is concerned, the total volume of cargo handled by this new service in its first year of operation (165,000 TEUs) accounted for only 1.1% of the container throughput in Hong Kong over the same period.[22] Taken together these findings indicate that Fixed-Point Direct Shipping across the Taiwan Strait is unlikely to constitute a serious threat to

---

[21] As in note 18.
[22] Census and Statistics Department, Hong Kong SAR Government, *Hong Kong Economic Trend*, August 1998, p. 3.

the development of Hong Kong's re-export business in the near future.

However, if the partial link were, for whatever reasons, to be developed into full-scale direct shipping — that is, the resumption of *san tong* — then its impact would be quite different. Maritime trade experts in the region have estimated that as much as 38% of Hong Kong's re-export business would probably be diverted away from Hong Kong in a short period following any resumption of *san tong*.[23] Therefore, the real threat to Hong Kong's re-export trade, the growth engine of its external trade, is not the potential loss of a proportion of re-exports between China and Taiwan, but rather the possible diversion of a substantial proportion of re-exports between China and foreign countries away from Hong Kong to Taiwan's ports, chiefly Kaohsiung.

Conclusions

This chapter has discussed the potential impact on Hong Kong's re-export trade, as a consequence of the resumption of *san tong* across the Taiwan Strait. In summary, as far as re-exports between China and Taiwan are concerned, the impact is likely to be minimal, because such movements only account for 7% of Hong Kong's total re-export trade, and about half of such re-exports would likely continue to be moved via Hong Kong after the resumption of *san tong* in any case. In terms of re-exports between China and foreign countries, however, the impact would be substantial — an estimated 38% of such movements could be diverted to Taiwanese ports in the short term following *san tong*. However, this loss is likely to be regained with the gradual increase in business from China over the long term. Thus, while Hong Kong's re-export trade may have

---

[23] Ling Yun, "The oriental pearl is still shining", p. 56.

survived the handover, the real challenge to its position as one of the world's leading *entrepôt* centres is posed by the possible resumption of direct trading linkages across the Taiwan Strait.

Chapter 4
HONG KONG'S TRANSITION: A VIEW FROM INDONESIA

Jusuf WANANDI

Introduction

In the brief period since Hong Kong became a Special Administrative Region (SAR) of the PRC much has happened. While it is perhaps still too early to make a substantive evaluation about Hong Kong's development and future, it is worthwhile to see what has actually changed and how much Hong Kong has developed since the transfer. Such an assessment is best undertaken in relation to the expectations about the changes before the transfer of authority from the British to China. This chapter will examine the changes in Hong Kong since China regained sovereignty from an Indonesian perspective.

Indonesia's policy towards Hong Kong has always been based on two premises. First, that Hong Kong is very much a part of China. Second, that Hong Kong is an important gateway to China and has been very useful as Indonesia's economic partner in East Asia, particularly in trade and investment. Indonesia has always expected that China would regain sovereignty over Hong Kong. However, as a Special Administrative Region, and in view of Hong Kong's special achievements including on the political front during the last few years prior to the transfer of authority, Hong Kong should be given some leeway in pursuing her own political development. Of course, this should be undertaken within the constraints of Chinese sovereignty, and within the SAR status of Hong Kong. These notions of Chinese sovereignty and the special status of the SAR have not yet been clearly defined in relation to each other.

Events since the Transfer

Indonesia itself has been undergoing dramatic changes since the onset of the economic crisis which coincided with the transfer of Hong Kong in July 1997. Persistent arguments about the need for political reform in Indonesia have returned recently in the context of the current traumatic upheaval. Developments on the political front have deeply affected views on the need for political change to be undertaken in Indonesia as early as possible. Such circumstances in Indonesia have reemphasized the critical underlying position such reforms must play in a country's national development strategy. The so-called "Korean model" of economic development first and political development later is no longer valid because this strategy only hampers the possibility of any meaningful political development. Ultimately, the cost of postponement is much higher. This is due to the enormous cost of political change after a long period of denial or suppression. The case of Indonesia demonstrates that the cost of delayed political reforms can be so much greater than the benefits of 30 years of sustained rapid economic growth.

Hong Kong as a SAR of China is of course a special case (*sui generis*). As such Hong Kong embodies its own ideas about, and rules on political development that should not be neglected. While there have been limits to political developments in the Hong Kong SAR, Hong Kong has successfully retained freedom of expression, information, organization and even the opportunity to elect some of its own representatives in the Legislature. Also, the freedom of movement has been kept intact. These rights have been in existence since before the transfer of authority by the British.

Most attention prior to the transfer focused on political developments since a majority of observers, particularly among the Western media, were concerned about whether the SAR would be granted the authority by China to exercise political rights and freedoms. In fact, most observers now agree that there have been no calamities on the issues of political rights and freedoms. The re-election of the leader of the Democratic Party, Martin Lee, who is the most consistent critic of China's policies towards Hong Kong attests to this situation. Mr. Lee's reelection was achieved with a clear majority of votes and along with him, the Democratic Party has gained a majority of seats among the elected members of the Legislative Council (Legco). Meanwhile, concerns about press-freedom, freedom of expression, and the right to organize have eased in the period since the transfer. In general terms, China has lived up to its promise not to interfere with the developments and policies of the Hong Kong SAR, especially on the political front. This is widely considered as critical to maintaining the credibility of the SAR and the one China and two systems idea of Deng Xiaoping.

Current criticisms of the SAR focus mainly on economic performance and policies which have resulted in unemployment, high interest rates, and the tumbling of share and real estate prices. Moreover, the government has been unlucky since the transfer having to cope with a series of incidents such as outbreaks of the bird flu and cholera, pollution of beaches, and especially the mishandling of the opening of the new airport. More than anything else, the accusation is that the government consists mostly of a former bureaucratic elite that has never been exposed to notions of accountability, but rather demonstrates all the trappings of an aloofness and arrogance to public responsibility. The last reshuffling of the government officials was meant to rectify this.

The intervention in the stock exchange in early August 1998 to prevent short-term speculation could have been avoided if the government and the bureaucracy had listened to the advice and criticisms of the academic and private sectors regarding obvious loopholes in the norms and regulations that were expressed as early as in February 1998. Instead, in April the government produced a report suggesting that everything was fine and that there was no need for changes in the regulatory environment of the stock exchange. This view, of course, backfired, when the inadequacies and loopholes were exploited by speculators in July and early August, 1998. This would have been a bigger blow for the Hong Kong administration and its laissez faire policies, had the subsequent response not been viewed in relation to the intervention by the Federal Reserve of New York in the case of the Long Term Capital Management hedge fund that September. Even still, such a massive intervention in the market could easily be criticized as an abandoning of capitalist principles, looking more like Malaysia which imposed currency controls only a few weeks later.

Still, the most important factor in Hong Kong's future, namely China, has largely kept its bargain with respect to the SAR by keeping itself very much in the background. Speculation was rife, for instance, that the Hong Kong government had consulted China on the market intervention in August 1998 and that it had received support. Indeed, if this was the case, such consultation was undertaken discreetly and did not become a real factor, as was acknowledged later even by Martin Lee. Also important now, in the aftermath of its intervention, is how the SAR will manage the 10–15 billion US dollars of shares that it acquired as a result of its foray into the market. Others have speculated that the government intervened partly as a result of its collusion, perceived since well before the transfer, with the "fat-cats" of Hong Kong. To a certain extent, however, this has always been an accepted fact by the local populace.

The Chief Executive, Mr. Tung Chee Hwa, who has lost some of his popularity recently, while considered a good man, is perceived as a novice in the job. The people of Hong Kong expect that his performance will improve with his second year in office. Equally important for the future, is how the Tung Chee Hwa-led government is going to fulfill the promises made at the beginning of his term, particularly in an array of fields that were neglected under British colonial rule: public housing; reforms to the education system that has declined and is vital for Hong Kong's future competitiveness, and; social security for the elderly and poor. Due to the current economic difficulties most of these promises have not been adequately addressed.

The idea of investing in Hong Kong's future to become another high-tech centre in East Asia is definitely critical for Hong Kong's future. In addition, Hong Kong will continue as a financial centre only with considerable effort since Singapore has been undertaking all the necessary regulatory initiatives to reform its financial system to compete directly with Hong Kong. On the other hand, Hong Kong's laudable reputation as a capitalist centre has taken a beating due to government intervention in the equity market in August 1998. Hong Kong needs to ensure that this will not happen again. In addition to rectifying the shortcomings in the financial system that were exploited by short-term funds speculators, the SAR must strengthen the attractiveness of other financial services. While recent land auctions in Hong Kong indicated some positive signs, the administration must also address the long term health of the real estate market.

The other sector now beginning to receive some considerable attention is the development of high-technology. While this initiative is perhaps a little too late, it is better than never. Hong Kong has for too long been focused on performing the role of a trading entrêpot for China. Since China will increasingly undertake its trade directly with the rest of the world, Hong Kong must consider how it can best reposition its role in the wider region. Hong Kong has the advantage of being in a good position to attract talent of Chinese origin, especially those trained abroad and who have had difficulty finding overseas employment. The development of human resources is critical for the advancement of high-tech industries and Hong Kong has all the ingredients to be able to attract talents from all over the world.

The Importance of Hong Kong in East Asia

Hong Kong as part of China is important to East Asia in particular and the world in general as a key gateway to Mainland China. With its special status for 50 years, Hong Kong will continue the process of internationalization and good governance based on the rule of law, and could serve as a model of development to be emulated by the rest of China. The role of Hong Kong for the wider East Asian region and for China is apparent in at least five important ways. First, China still needs the capabilities and acumen of Hong Kong as a trading and a financial centre. Despite renewed emphasis on building capacity in Shanghai, Hong Kong will continue to provide a much better administrative and legal environment, with a transparency and related freedoms that are necessary for a vibrant economy to be able to respond effectively to the vagaries globalization. Regional corporate headquarters have been established in Hong Kong to invest in China particularly for these reasons.

However, there is a sense that under the provisions of the Basic Law and other legislation introduced earlier by the British government, and as a SAR of China, political development in Hong Kong has been somewhat muted. It is important to emphasize again that Hong Kong has to retain and develop some sense of participatory politics in addition to the political rights and freedoms that Hong Kong residents currently enjoy. China is particularly well disposed to allow that to happen, as long as this does not lead to chaos in Hong Kong and that circumstances do not conspire to subvert the Chinese political system. For this to happen, there needs to be an improvement in the relationship between the Executive and the Legislative Branches. Both branches have the responsibility to encourage participatory politics in Hong Kong. A merely legalistic approach is no longer adequate. Statesmanship and political acumen is required on both sides as well as a willingness to implement workable compromises acceptable to both the people of Hong Kong and the government of China.

Achieving such political compromise will require some kind of creative ambiguity. As a businessman, Tung Chee Hwa should see this as a long-term business proposition where both sides have to make a profit to make the deal palatable to both. Politics involves the art of compromise. The opposition in the Legislative Branch should appreciate that only a political compromise will be acceptable to China, and that the willingness of China to go along will be a vital element in Hong Kong's future. If this could be achieved in the next few years, then the Hong Kong model of good governance and political development could also influence the future political situation in China. Of course, participatory politics is not the only important part of political development and democracy in Hong Kong. Other political rights such as freedom of expression, organization, and movement are equally important. Although these rights are already guaranteed in Hong Kong, they should be guarded constantly because they can easily be lost.

The rule of law is of paramount importance in a democracy and is a vital part of good governance. The rule of law and the integrity of the courts in Hong Kong should be maintained so as to sustain the trust of international and local businesses. This is what differentiates Hong Kong from all the other parts of China, including Shanghai.

Second, China could learn from Hong Kong on how to cope with the processes of globalization and on the gradual trends of political opening up and development. This is vital for the region since one of the biggest challenges is how China will cope with such trends. If Hong Kong can continue as a critical gateway and serve as a model of development for China, this relationship secures Hong Kong's role in the region as well. From this perspective, Indonesian relations with Hong Kong should be established, maintained and increased.

Third, only if the Hong Kong SAR survives and thrives over the next five years or so, will Taiwan pay any serious attention to the idea of "one country two systems" as proposed by Mainland China as a basis for the process of negotiating reunification. Taiwan must also consider the *modus vivendi* with China over the longer term after China has become more democratic. Meanwhile, Taiwan has to find ways to respond to various kinds of pressures exerted by the Mainland. Stable relations between China and Taiwan are necessary for the stability of the region. Hong Kong could play an indirect though very important part in the process of identifying viable strategies for securing stable relations between China and Taiwan over the medium term. While reunification between Taiwan and China will not be the same as the return of Hong Kong, a compromise may be more likely if the formula applied to Hong Kong proves viable over the medium term.

Fourth, Hong Kong's importance as a trading centre for the region and as a source for financing and other services is significant not only for China, but also for Southeast Asia including Indonesia. Hong Kong is now the fourth largest investor in Indonesia with a value of almost 14 billion US dollars at the end of 1997. As discussed above, Hong Kong must maintain its international credibility in order to retain its status as a successful trading and financial centre. Government intervention in the equity market in the summer of 1998 is not helpful to Hong Kong's credibility.

Meanwhile, many Indonesian companies have branches in Hong Kong as part of their strategy to utilize Hong Kong's proximity to China and as a gateway to the Chinese market. In addition, by establishing corporate entities in Hong Kong Indonesian companies gain access to financing from Hong Kong to invest in China. Their presence in the former colony allows them to become acquainted with Chinese enterprises operating in Hong Kong some of whom are potential partners for entry into the Chinese market.

Fifth, Hong Kong has become an important member of regional institutions such as APEC, PECC, and PBEC. These institutions are playing an important role in the creation of an Asia Pacific community. Stemming from a consistent emphasis on free trade (notwithstanding the recent intervention in the financial market), Hong Kong has played a constructive and creative role in these institutions, which augurs well for its regional and international economic relations. As an important player in the East Asian and wider Asia Pacific region, active participation in such regional bodies secures Hong Kong's position as a significant economic entity in the international community. Hong Kong should be prepared to invest more in these regional institutions. This should not only be manifested at the government level, but perhaps more so at the track two level, such as in PECC or PBEC, since participation in the deliberations, networking, and studies undertaken in these fora are more intense, informal, and useful.

Conclusion

Indonesia has had a productive relationship with Hong Kong. Previously, Hong Kong served as the main window from which to observe China. However, this is no longer the case, since direct relations between China and Indonesia have prospered. Nonetheless, Hong Kong remains a very important economic interlocutor between China and Indonesia despite the establishment of direct relations. In fact, Hong Kong has acted as an effective bridge between China and Indonesia over a long period. This is likely to be the case for some time since China is still a difficult place to invest for Indonesia and also vice versa.

Hong Kong's importance for Indonesia and the rest of Southeast Asia is more than just in terms of economic relations. Hong Kong is also important politically and strategically, however indirect. Therefore, there must be more intellectual discourse and cooperation between Hong Kong and Southeast Asia. Since most activities on the political front will be limited to track one initiatives, academic and similar kinds of cooperation should be undertaken and developed via track two endeavours. This will be important for all sides.

Hong Kong simultaneously embodies an array of local, Chinese, East Asian and global characteristics. Such multiple identities are a new phenomenon which have arisen mainly due to globalization. Sovereignty is no longer an absolute. It is mitigated by regionalism and globalization (such as through APEC or the UN), the rise of localism (more autonomy, decentralization, more rights for minorities, etc.), and by the emergence of civil society (NGOs, the private sector, think tanks, the press, etc. both inside and outside the country). These circumstances pose new challenges for a strong state like

China. China can learn from Hong Kong's experience as she grapples with such multiple identities. Furthermore, since China has not yet fully opened its economy, this makes Hong Kong all the more important as a potential model for the Mainland. Lastly, it seems that Hong Kong will continue to play an important role in the region. As such, Indonesia must continue to pay attention to the circumstances of Hong Kong's transition well into the future.

Chapter 5
HONG KONG'S TRANSITION: A VIEW FROM MALAYSIA

Stephen LEONG[1]

Introduction

On the night of 30 June 1997, Malaysians joined the global community in witnessing the long-awaited historic reversion of Hong Kong to China. The occasion marked the territory's independence from colonial rule just before the present century draws to a close. Malaysians are well aware of the expansion of British imperialism in East Asia as a result of the infamous Opium War (1839–42) which ended with the cessation of Hong Kong to Britain. While Malaya, itself a British colony, was able to gain *merdeka* in 1957, Hong Kong, a glaring anachronism of Western colonialism in Asia, was not to be freed until a good 40 years later. From the outset, therefore, Malaysians had hoped that the transition of Hong Kong as a British colony to Chinese rule as a Special Administrative Region (SAR) in China would be a success.

---

[1] The views expressed in this chapter are those of the author alone.

This positive attitude is also due to the vigorous debate among world observers, as was well reflected in the international media, on Hong Kong's future after reversion to China. As is well-known, huge doubts have been raised concerning the new Hong Kong administration's ability to run the territory efficiently, especially to be free of corruption and to be assured of the continuity of the rule of law.

Having also experienced lengthy British colonial rule, Malaysians could readily identify with the residents of Hong Kong and wish them success in the post-colonial transition as a region of China. As Tun Daim Zainuddin, Special Economic Advisor to the Malaysian Government, observed a few days before the historic handover: "Given the common heritage of British legal and administrative institutions, Malaysia will be able to interact smoothly with Hong Kong in its new role. A further factor enhancing the overall interaction between Malaysia and Hong Kong is the excellent relationship that Malaysia and the People's Republic of China have so carefully nurtured over the past few decades. Since the visit in 1974 of the then-prime minister Tun Abdul Razak, Malaysia and China have developed a relationship that can be considered a model in terms of bilateral ties."[2]

Malaysians are optimistic that the SAR will succeed in its transition because of its well-trained civil service which had amply demonstrated its capabilities under British rule. Just as Malaysia was able to cope with challenges during its own transition four decades earlier without the British around, Hong Kong's administration will also be able do so. The premium for success is especially high with world attention focused on the prospects for Hong Kong's future. Watching the

---

[2] Tun Daim Zainuddin, "Hong Kong 1997: Business After the Handover" (The View from Abroad), *Asian Business*. http://web3.asial.com.sg/timesnet/datahk97/intro.html #intr.

spectacular and smoothly-executed handing over ceremony on television at midnight on 30 June 1997, Malaysians perceived an unmistakable air of confidence in Hong Kong. They felt assured that the SAR would perform well.

Who could have imagined that Hong Kong would be set upon by a series of unprecedented travails soon after the historic reversion to China? "Baptism by fire" would most suitably describe the events that ensued. From health hazards — avian (chicken) flu, contaminated fish or "red tide", a cholera outbreak and pesticide-tainted vegetables — Hong Kong is now faced with its worst recession since World War II. The barrage of problems have prompted SAR detractors to comment that "the government's poor response to a string of non-economic foul-ups ... has contributed to a growing sense that this administration is both less competent and less responsive to the public than was the colonial government."[3] However, Malaysian support for Hong Kong continued in the face of the crisis because Kuala Lumpur (like other Asian capitals) was also encountering hitherto unfamiliar hardship. Hong Kong's problems have become part and parcel of the wider Asian regional economic malaise. Malaysia can, therefore, readily identify with Hong Kong and render moral support in its present predicament. This chapter will provide a Malaysian perspective on the transition of Hong Kong to China.

Political and Administrative Change and Continuity

Malaysia has been closely watching developments in Hong Kong from the time of the Sino-British Joint Declaration in 1984 until the handover in 1997. Malaysians felt that the souring of relations

---

[3] Bretigne Shafter "Hong Kong's Quest for Accountability", *Asian Wall Street Journal* (AWSJ), 22 September 1997.

between the Hong Kong government and Chinese authorities in Beijing over the last few years of British rule was largely due to Governor Chris Patten's insistence on promoting legislative reforms and democracy before reversion to China. Why did the British choose to promote democracy in Hong Kong only during the twilight years of its century-and-a-half rule? Malaysians were cynical that the people of Hong Kong were not entitled to democracy under the British because of the concern that it would undermine colonial power and status in Hong Kong. Despite steadfast objections from Beijing to Patten's intention to hastily promote democracy, thus straining Sino-British relations as well as the Chinese central government's ties with the colony's residents, the British governor remained determined to go ahead with unilateral reforms for the Hong Kong Legislature.

As the issue of leadership was crucial for Hong Kong's successful transition, Malaysians generally understood Beijing's need to appoint someone with whom they could work as head of the SAR. Tung Chee Hwa was regarded as a leader acceptable to both Beijing and the residents of Hong Kong. The Provisional Legislature, which on 1 July 1997 replaced the Legislative Council set up earlier under British rule, was deemed legitimate since the previous colonial government-sponsored body was known to have been established against strong objections from Beijing on the grounds that it contravened the 1984 Sino-British Joint Declaration on Hong Kong.

Owing to Hong Kong residents' inclination for greater freedom, it was anticipated that the pro-democracy political parties would win much of the popular vote in the first elections in post-handover Hong Kong in May 1998. While Malaysians understand the desire of the Hong Kong people to safeguard their interests by promoting democracy, they are also mindful of the community's active role during the 1989 Tiananmen unrest. Conscious of the racial riots that wreaked havoc in their own country 30 years ago, Malaysians have since given top priority to political stability. The country's sterling economic performance since 1969 attests to peace and stability as an indispensable prerequisite for economic development. Malaysian concern is that while Hong Kong would have little difficulty dealing with democracy, it is unclear if Beijing would be able to manage the consequences on the larger Chinese society. Many mainland Chinese might be keen to emulate Hong Kong's democratic movement. With their predilection for a peaceful and evolutionary path for developing democracy and civil society, Malaysians can appreciate Beijing's concern about political developments in the SAR.

On the pertinent issue of the central government's relations with the SAR after the handover, Beijing has done well in abiding by the Basic Law and the "one country two systems" formula. It has not undertaken any action to undermine the independence of the SAR. As the *Far Eastern Economic Review* analyst, Frank Ching, recently observed, "[i]n fact, in the 15 months since the change in sovereignty, rights and freedom have not been curbed, and both China and Hong Kong have insisted that the SAR authorities have been exercising full autonomy, aside from defence and foreign affairs."[4]

Economic Change and Continuity

Hong Kong's legendary dynamism and reputation as the world's freest economy have long been acknowledged by Malaysians. In assessing its fundamentals on the eve of the reversion to Chinese rule, Tun Daim Zainuddin noted that Hong Kong's US$42 billion in foreign currency reserves "creates a solid underpinning for Hong Kong's future prosperity."[5] While Hong Kong's reserves are bigger

---

[4] Frank Ching, "Hong Kong Needs Openness", *Far Eastern Economic Review* (FEER), 8 October 1998, p. 89.

[5] Tun Daim Zainuddin, op. cit.

than those of many countries, economists still caution that the SAR's structural shift in manufacturing activities since the mid-1980s, and, as we shall see later, the apparent vulnerability of its financial system to speculative attacks, warrant guarded optimism rather than over-confidence for Hong Kong's future.

On Hong Kong's role in the regional economy, Tun Daim expressed confidence that a capitalist, market-driven economy like Hong Kong would enrich and expand the market-driven economic systems both in Southeast and East Asia. He saw avenues for economic cooperation and business synergies between Malaysian and Hong Kong entrepreneurs. The Malaysian leader elaborated that "the post-1997 scenario in Hong Kong could provide the foundation for Sino-Malay joint ventures on a global scale. As Malaysia develops rapidly towards its goal of achieving a developed and fully democratic society, the transition of Hong Kong from British colonialism can only be a factor for peace and prosperity in Malaysia-China relations and in the wider Asia-Pacific context."[6]

Amidst the financial and economic crisis which has beset Asian countries since July 1997, events in Hong Kong since the handover have unfolded fortuitously in Malaysia's favour. What appeared to be competing attention for the almost simultaneous official opening of the new Kuala Lumpur International Airport (KLIA) and Hong Kong's Chek Lap Kok Airport (CLK), turned out to be a blessing for Malaysia. Up until the CLK's launch on 6 July, the KLIA (official opening on 28 June) received a heavy dose of criticism because of the teething problems encountered. The bad press was soon deflected when the international media began to focus on ground operations at CLK. By comparison, the CLK woes were far worse than those of the KLIA. While empathising with Hong Kong, Malaysians also breathed a sigh of relief for the CLK's

---

[6] *Ibid.*

unwitting role in deflecting the unwanted attention on the plight of the KLIA.

Although Hong Kong might view it differently, for Malaysia, the SAR's direct intervention against currency attack and stock market speculation in August 1998 was heaven-sent. The actions of the Hong Kong government undoubtedly strengthened Prime Minister Mahathir Mohamad's moves against international currency speculators to eliminate the volatility in exchange-rates which had a devastating impact on regional stock markets and financial systems. Championing the Malaysian response since September 1997, the Prime Minister and fellow countrymen fully welcomed SAR Secretary Anson Chan's comments on attacks on the Hong Kong dollar and the stock market: "We cannot tolerate somebody creating confusion in the foreign exchange market, damaging our system, the interests of our businessmen and the public."[7] As early as 23 October 1997, a Malaysian *Business Times* editorial titled *A Tragic Asian Drama* had warned, "as the Prime Minister has pointed out, this is no time to keep quiet in the hope — a delusive one, one might add — that the speculators would not notice you when they select their next victim. Developments have shown that no one will be spared; not the mighty Singapore dollar, not the Taiwan dollar, not even the Hong Kong stock market with its enviable buffer of resources and business opportunities that mainland China promises."

Ten months later, with some vindication, the same Malaysian daily commented that "finally, Hong Kong, the world's free market bastion, has called for order in the international financial market. It took Asia's financial hub only a couple of weeks of relentless attacks by the currency speculators to admit that the free market in its current form is no longer tenable." The newspaper was pleased to note that Financial Secretary, Sir Donald Tsang, had called for a

---

[7] *New Straits Times,* 17 August 1998.

global plan to discipline financial markets and control the flow of funds, suggesting that the countries in Asia as well as the International Monetary Fund (IMF) must reach a consensus on how to proceed with the proposal. Malaysia would certainly support Hong Kong's call for a global plan to discipline speculators as the proposal was not too different from what Dr. Mahathir had been suggesting to Asia and the world since September 1997.[8]

Malaysian defence of what might be regarded as a common cause and support for the SAR in its efforts to stave of efforts to weaken the Hong Kong dollar and stock market was best illustrated by the response of the Deputy Head of the UMNO Youth wing, Hishammudin Tun Hussein to the *Asian Wall Street Journal* (*AWSJ*) editorial titled "Hong Kong Blunder" of 17 August 1998 harshly criticising Financial Secretary, Sir Donald Tsang, and the Hong Kong Monetary Authority (HKMA) for intervening in the stock market. The *AWSJ* critique began as follows: "Donald Tsang and Mahathir Mohamad. Nobody ever thought to group the Hong Kong financial secretary and Malaysia's prime minister together in the same league. Until last Friday." Reacting to the *AWSJ* commentary, Hishammudin elaborated: "I would like to point out that the recent simultaneous attack on the Hong Kong dollar and its stock market only serve to underscore a point that Dr. Mahathir has frequently made to little avail: that currency speculators, like locusts, are highly indiscriminate. Not only are they borderless, they are remorseless and, as Malaysia has good reason to know, completely ruthless in pursuing their profit-oriented objectives." The Malaysian youth leader further argued that the attack on Hong Kong and Russia underscored the point — that a country's ability to craft economic policy and monetary policy to serve its own national interest can be usurped by what the *AWSJ* was pleased to call "free market forces".

---

[8] "The Fall of the Free Market", *Business Times*, 10 September 1998.

Hishammudin emphasized that it was one thing for an economist to criticize government policy. However, when criticism by a currency speculator was supported by the power of huge and highly leveraged funds to reinforce their views, their criticisms should rightly be called something else. He maintained that it was a fallacy to speak of the wisdom of the marketplace when regulators like the Securities and Exchange Commission in the U.S. saw fit to institute circuit breakers in the aftermath of the October 1991 stock market plunge, and when the London Stock Exchange changed the rules immediately after Malaysia's PNB Corporation made a successful dawn raid on Guthrie's in 1981. The Malaysian leader questioned the *AWSJ*'s wisdom in labelling Hong Kong's currency intervention in the stock market "a blunder" when both actions were implicit recognition that markets needed occasional guidance and cannot always be allowed unfettered freedom, especially when imperfect human beings cannot make perfect decisions all the time.[9]

Anxious for the international community to act on currency speculation, Malaysians were somewhat disappointed when the local press reported on 19 October 1998 that despite the worrisome encounter with hedge fund attacks on the Hong Kong dollar and stock market, Sir Donald Tsang proposed that no regulations be imposed on the speculators until full knowledge of their operations is obtained. To do otherwise would be an "overreaction." The SAR official, however, proposed that "central bankers, hedge fund owners as well as the business and banking sectors, should get together and work out a system whereby we can collect more information and have a deeper knowledge of how hedge funds operate .... We need to start the dialogue as soon as possible but those responsible for regulation must not overreact." Tsang urged the financial institutions such as banks to lend prudently to hedge funds so as to

---

[9] "Letter to the Editor", *AWSJ*, 4–5 September 1998.

avoid a systemic problem and called for codified practices on the transparency and disclosure of investment funds positions. He added that issues relating to prudent lending by banks should be properly discussed as soon as possible through the Bank of International Settlement.[10]

Regarding the Chinese central government's stand on the currency and stock market crisis besetting Hong Kong, Malaysians were pleased with Beijing's announcement that it would utilise its reserves to shore up Hong Kong's defence against currency speculators if requested to do so by the SAR Administration.[11] Indeed, Hong Kong can consider itself fortunate that it can rely on such strong financial backing. Malaysians also understand the reluctance on the part of the SAR to request Beijing's assistance at this stage of the crisis since such recourse could be interpreted as an inability of the post-handover administration to safeguard the interests of Hong Kong's business community. Such a move could also be perceived as central government interference in the affairs of the SAR, thus compromising the one country two systems formula for Hong Kong's post-reversion transition. Beijing probably took into consideration the Taiwan factor. Despite Taiwan's rejection of one country two systems for its reunification process with the Mainland, and its strong aversion to currency speculation, Taipei might still regard Beijing's possible intervention as contrary to its commitments to the independence of the SAR.

Therefore, with respect to the SAR-central government relationship, Malaysians would disagree with Nobel laureate Milton Friedman's reaction to the HKMA's intervention in the stock market. Renowned for championing the free-market system, the American

---

[10] *New Straits Times,* 19 October 1998.
[11] Maggie Farley, "Rough Times Follow Hong Kong Handover", *Japan Times,* 3 July 1998.

economist expressed concern that as a part of China, Hong Kong's status was eroding. Having predicted earlier that the one country two systems policy would not last, Friedman opined that he was sorry to see such circumstances emerge sooner than expected.[12]

Looking Ahead

As the unique one country two systems formula continues into the new century, the interaction process between the two systems during the next 50 years or so will necessarily be one of give-and-take. This is so even as Hong Kong residents might be keen to respond to Legislative Council member Christine Loh Kung-wai's call to defend "Hong Kong culture" whose "defining qualities are its openness and pragmatism" compared to "the nationalism, patriotism and the dogmatism favoured by Peking."[13] To the extent that political developments in Hong Kong do not threaten (or are not perceived by Beijing to threaten) political and social stability on the mainland, Hong Kong can continue to be administered by its own people. Given that present-day China is still in the midst of an evolutionary transition towards more "openness", a compromise solution would most likely be achieved by both sides for Hong Kong's position in China after July 2047. One country two systems could effectively evolve into one country one system. This perspective takes into consideration the Taiwan-Mainland China equation. Considering the more complex reunification process, and Taipei's relative strength (compared to Hong Kong relations with Beijing), Malaysians would not be surprised if a sovereign "Greater China," emerged with a federal system of government as the most realistic outcome for all

---

[12] "Nobel Laureate Hits Hong Kong for Share Buys", *AWSJ*, 3 September 1998.
[13] Christine Loh Kung-wai, "The Making of the History of Modern China — Hong Kong's Contribution", *Asian Perspective* (Spring 1995), p. 2.

parties concerned. In view of the intractable nature of the problem, particularly the Mainland-Taiwan relationship, such a system would very likely win support from the international community.

Looking ahead to Hong Kong's future and its ties with economies throughout the region, Tun Daim Zainuddin observed earlier that "the positive long-term view is to see Hong Kong's date with destiny as marking the turning point and the catalyst for a more fruitful, more intense collaboration between the business communities of Malaysia and China .... While there has been a lot of discussion about capital flight from Hong Kong, and about businesses relocating because of the handover, Malaysia views this as a temporary phenomenon. In no way is this likely to cloud the strong bonds of friendship and cooperation between Malaysia and China."[14]

Malaysia-China relations have indeed been positive especially since the beginning of this decade with growing bilateral trade and investment and China's support of the Malaysian initiative for the East Asian Economic Caucus. Kuala Lumpur and other ASEAN capitals hit hard by the economic crisis have also been very appreciative of Beijing's assurance that the *yuan* would not be devalued so that further competitive depreciation or devaluation of other regional currencies could be averted.

As for Malaysia-Hong Kong relations, like other ASEAN nations, Malaysia will continue to regard the SAR as a leading financial centre and a major gateway and bridge to China. This view is held despite concerns by some that owing to its rapid development, Shanghai would replace Hong Kong as China's financial centre by the mid-21st Century. However, Malaysians feel that Chairman and CEO of Bank of East Asia David K. P. Li's view that "an economy the size of China's will support at least a dozen major financial centres, each developing a niche in accordance with geography and

---

[14] Tun Daim Zainuddin, op. cit.

tradition",[15] is overly optimistic for China. Even though Singapore and Tokyo will continue to compete with Hong Kong, following the current crisis and the reemergence and expansion of Asia's economy in the years ahead, such established cities could also serve as complementary financial centres in East Asia. In this context Malaysians are optimistic that even newcomer Labuan (in Sabah) will be able to find a valuable niche in the new century.

As the Hong Kong SAR integrates with Mainland China within the one country two systems framework, it will also continue to forge closer links with other regional economies and the wider global community through multilateral organisations such as APEC and the WTO. Long regarded as the model for free trade *par excellence*, Hong Kong served notice that it would press for progress in trade liberalisation at the last APEC meeting in Kuala Lumpur. Although the developed economies of APEC (except Japan) wished to advance on the nine early voluntary sectors for liberalisation, and Malaysia urged the regional body to act swiftly on the current financial crisis, Cherry Ling, Hong Kong's Acting Director-General of Trade was of the view that "trade liberalisation can help solve the financial crisis."[16] As the Hong Kong administration has identified electronic commerce and information technology as new growth areas for Hong Kong's future development, these were emphasized by the SAR at the APEC forum.[17]

Hong Kong's targeting of e-commerce and IT for its own development and growth, as well as upgrading competitiveness in the regional and global arena is very much in line with the goals of Malaysia's own Multimedia Super Corridor development aimed at

---

[15] David K. P. Li, "China in 2046", *Far Eastern Economic Review 50th Anniversary Issue* (1997), p. 188.
[16] *Business Times*, 22 October 1998.
[17] *Ibid.*

propelling the country into the information-technology world of the next century. Given the new and expansive horizons for development of high technologies and the growing necessity to be wired into the regional and global economies, rather than viewing such common visions in a competitive context, the potential for complimentarity and cooperation should be emphasized. Just as free and fair commerce has served regional and global economies well in the past, the international community should strive to ensure that it continues to do so in the future.

Conclusion

The first year of the post-handover period was truly *annus horribilis* for Hong Kong. In the context of the region-wide financial crisis, Malaysians can fully empathise with the SAR's predicament. Like Hong Kong, which celebrated the end of colonial rule and became part of a sovereign China in July 1997, Malaysia too was euphoric as it celebrated 40 years of independence the same year. Together with other ASEAN countries, Malaysians also proudly hailed the 30th anniversary of the regional body. Along with Hong Kong, most regional economies were highly acclaimed as the "East Asian Miracle". Then came the tidal wave. Within the context of the handover to China, and given the fact that no one could have predicted the speed and extent of the regional financial and economic crisis, the Hong Kong administration might have been expected to respond somewhat differently to a range of difficult circumstances. However, from a Malaysian perspective, except for the CLK fiasco, it could be said that Hong Kong performed creditably in its first year after the handover. More significantly, in view of the deep pessimism expressed by some (generally the West) concerning China's adherence to the one country two systems formula, Beijing should also be credited for abiding by its promises.

On the issue most pertinent to Malaysia — the problem of currency speculation in what has now become a global crisis — Malaysians have supported the SAR's intervention in the stock market. There existed an overriding need for swift action to avert a market collapse and to ensure the stability of the Hong Kong dollar. Prevention is still better than cure, especially when the currency and stock market crisis can wreak havoc on the real economy thus affecting the livelihood of untold masses of Hong Kong residents.

Finally, despite Hong Kong's year of travails, Malaysians remain optimistic about its ability to survive. Most would concur with the Chairman of the Trade Development Council, Victor Fung, when he said, "[s]ure, we need to invent ourselves again .... But Hong Kong has repeatedly done this in the past."[18]

APPENDIX

Summary of Hong Kong's Trade with Malaysia

Value in HK$ million

	July 1996 - June 1997	July 1997 - June 1998	% Change July-June 1998/97
Domestic Exports	2,586	2,334	-9.8
Re-exports	10,430	9,934	-4.8
Imports	36,992	35,559	-3.9
Total Trade	50,008	47,827	-4.4
Balance of Trade	-23,976	-23,291	

Source: Hong Kong Trade Statistics, Hong Kong Economic & Trade Office, Singapore

[18] "Built to Last", *Newsweek,* 13 July 1998, p. 13.

Summary of Hong Kong's Trade with ASEAN*

Value in HK$ million

	July 1996 - June 1997	July 1997 - June 1998	% Change July-June 1998/97
Domestic Exports	18,762	15,134	-19.3
Re-exports	76,094	70,448	-7.4
Imports	164,916	159,786	-3.1
Total Trade	259,772	245,368	-5.5
Balance of Trade	-70,060	-74,204	

* *Figures do not include Laos and Myanmar (who joined ASEAN on 23 July 1997) and Cambodia (who joined on 30 April, 1999).*

Source: Hong Kong Statistics, Hong Kong Economic & Trade Office, Singapore

Chapter 6
HONG KONG'S TRANSITION: A VIEW FROM THAILAND

UMPHON Phanachet[1]

Introduction

As a departure from the traditional analytical approach to the issue of Hong Kong in transition, it is considered more appropriate from a Thai perspective to examine the issue over three different periods. The first is the pre-handover period, when various views and speculative scenarios were expounded — some pessimistic, others optimistic, and many pragmatic. The second is the period since the handover on 1 July 1997, during which the Hong Kong Special Administrative Region (SAR) encountered challenges and responded with remedial measures which have achieved some degree of success.

---

[1] The author wishes to record his appreciation for the comments made by Dr. Sheng Lijun of the Institute of Southeast Asian Studies, Singapore and other conference participants. The author is also grateful to Miss Punyacha Teparakul, Assistant Researcher, for the updating and finalizing of earlier drafts of this chapter. The views expressed here are those of the author alone.

The third period is the uncertain future of the Hong Kong SAR. This chapter will review each of these periods from a Thai perspective and conclude by proposing some possible areas of cooperation between Hong Kong and Southeast Asia.

The Reunification in Perspective

On 1 July 1997, world attention turned to the historic return of Hong Kong to China's sovereignty after more than 150 years under British rule. Since Hong Kong is one of the world's foremost trade and financial centres, such an event is of immense importance in Asia. Neighbouring Southeast Asian countries view the change of sovereignty and the related evolution of Hong Kong's future from a range of perspectives: pessimistic; optimistic; or pragmatic.

The pessimists argue, often with good reason, that civil rights and press freedom are unlikely to be maintained; corruption is sure to rise; the confidence of foreign businessmen is unlikely to be sustained for more than a couple of years; international competitiveness, including in the area of competence in the English language will gradually decline; the increased flow of illegal immigrants will inevitably cause higher crime rates and other social disorder — the list goes on. Some pessimists also do not rule out the possibility of political upheavals in China. These upheavals may not be on the same scale as the Cultural Revolution from 1966 to 1976, but could seriously affect trade, finance, communication, and other economic activities in Hong Kong. Increased competition from Southeast Asian countries and other Newly Industrialised Economies is inevitable. On the whole, many people seem to have less faith in Hong Kong's continued prosperity in the years to come. The fear of the loss of liberty and freedom after the handover was clearly reflected in the vast number of Hong Kong people who migrated to the USA, Canada, and Australia, especially after the Tiananmen incident. Although some of them later returned to Hong Kong, most have since obtained foreign passports.

By contrast, optimists base their views on the following, perhaps stronger arguments. First, there is absolutely no reason for China to intentionally or unintentionally kill the goose that lays China's golden eggs. Hong Kong has a significant impact on the economy of China. In terms of finance, China depends on Hong Kong to generate capital. For example, about 60% of total foreign investment in China originated or was directed from Hong Kong. Hong Kong is also China's largest trading partner. China also relies on and can learn from Hong Kong's advanced knowledge in technology, management, and marketing.

Second, China wants to demonstrate to the world that Hong Kong's economic growth and prosperity will continue under Chinese sovereignty. If Hong Kong's economy is hampered by the reunification, this will result in the loss of overseas investors' confidence, a negative effect on the mainland economy, and the loss of face on the world stage.

Third, China is hoping that Hong Kong's return under the "one country two systems" formula will work out successfully so that it can be utilized as a model for the peaceful reunification of Taiwan. Indeed, China is willing under such terms to grant Taiwan more autonomy than Hong Kong including retaining its own military forces and a Vice Presidential post in the Beijing administration for the "Chief Executive" of Taiwan. Southeast Asians of the Chinese ancestry know that both the Mainland and Taiwan share the same culture, history, and speak and write the same language. Only differences in political systems have kept them apart since 1949. The combined economic and financial strength arising from reunification would provide unprecedented bargaining power at the international level. Southeast Asian nations would also benefit from access to the widening international family of increasingly globalized economies. Moreover, the combined foreign exchange reserves of China, Hong Kong, and Taiwan could be used to invest in infrastructure and economic development in China, Southeast Asia, and South Asia.

Fourth, to ensure the continued success of Hong Kong, Beijing has repeatedly declared that it will not interfere with Hong Kong's domestic affairs and that it will not impose any dramatic changes for 50 years after the handover. China is determined to implement the Basic Law in Hong Kong to fulfill its international commitments and to provide a model solution for cross straits tensions. The Basic Law "included provisions for low taxes, universal suffrage by adults, and a chief executive and a legislature to be elected, first by select groups and eventually by the general public ... and stipulated that the SAR alone could decide how its taxes would be spent — the key to its past success — instead of having to share the funds with the rest of the country."[2]

Set against this largely optimistic background, and from a pragmatic Southeast Asian perspective on post-handover Hong Kong, it is important to remain cognizant of the following issues. It would be naive to assume that the handover will be smooth sailing for the Hong Kong SAR. Demands from pro-democracy groups led by personalities such as Mr. Martin Lee of the Democratic Party and Mrs. Christine Lo of the Citizens Party, and the high cost of business operations in Hong Kong will have to be tackled soon. Notoriously high real estate and rental prices, salaries, entertainment and other costs also require attention. Such negative phenomena invite challenges from Singapore, Malaysia, and Thailand. Meanwhile, the natural trend of capitalist management, lifestyles and outlook will continue to creep into China from Hong Kong, particularly into the Pearl River Delta and the nearby Special

---

[2] *Asiaweek*, 11 July 1997, p. 46.

Economic Zones. Similarly, Hong Kong will learn to understand more of the politics and management style of Chinese practices. Hopefully, each will absorb the finer qualities of the other. In addition, social and educational infrastructure in Hong Kong needs to be maintained in areas such as facility in the English language and the increasing use of Mandarin in place of the traditional Cantonese.

The Thailand–Hong Kong Relationship

(i) Pre-handover relations

Thailand and Hong Kong have maintained an excellent trading relationship. In spite of the financial crisis, there is every indication that trade between the two economies will continue to expand. In 1996, Thailand was Hong Kong's twelfth largest trading partner with total trade valued at some 121 billion Baht, an increase of more than 12% over 1995. A significant part of this trade stems from the export of Thai rice. In 1996, Thailand accounted for almost 77% of Hong Kong's total rice imports. Hong Kong is now Thailand's fifth largest overseas rice market.

As trading relations expand, Hong Kong entrepreneurs are coming to recognize the growing advantages of investing in Thailand. By the end of September 1995, Hong Kong became the second largest source of foreign investment in Thailand with subsequent inflows in 1996 reaching almost 50 billion Baht. Reciprocal flows positioned Thailand as the sixteenth largest investor in Hong Kong's non-manufacturing sector. At the same time there has been an increase in the number of people from Thailand who are living and working in Hong Kong. These figures illustrate the expanding ties between Thailand and Hong Kong and are indicative of the significant role each plays in the region.

As a large exporter of capital to the region, Hong Kong helps to generate prosperity, which in turn helps to bring greater political stability — a fact that has not gone unnoticed by the major European countries which have been turning their attention to the East Asian region in recent years. The establishment of the Asia-Europe summit with its inaugural meeting in Bangkok in 1996 serves to emphasize this point. In addition to investments in other countries throughout the region, Hong Kong is a source or conduit for about 60% of all investment going into China since 1978. Part of the significant Thai investments in China also went through Hong Kong.

(ii) Thailand and Hong Kong bilateral trade and investment

Tables 1 and 2, show Hong Kong's trade with ASEAN and bilateral trade with Thailand one year before and one year after 1 July 1997. As a result of the Asian financial crisis, total trade between Hong Kong and ASEAN fell by 5.5% from HK$259.8 billion to HK$245.4 billion. This resulted in an increase in the trade deficit from HK$70 billion over the year prior to 1 July 1997 to HK$74 billion for the one year period since the handover (see Table 1). By contrast, Thailand's bilateral trade with Hong Kong rose slightly from HK$38.5 billion to HK$38.8 billion over the same period (see Table 2). Meanwhile, Thailand's exports to Hong Kong rose by 7.5% from HK$23.9 billion to HK$25.7 billion and imports fell by 15% from HK$14.6 billion to HK$13.0 billion.[3] Thailand's exports to Hong Kong consisted primarily of light industrial products, agricultural and agro-industrial products. Thailand imported mostly manufactured goods and electronic products from Hong Kong.

---

[3] These figures were calculated from data in: Trade Statistics Center, Thai Department of Customs, 22 October 1998.

TABLE 1: Summary of Hong Kong's Trade with ASEAN[*]

Volume in HK$ million

	July 96 – June 97	July 97 – June 98	% Change July – June 98/97
Domestic Exports	18,762	15,134	-19.3
Re-exports	79,094	70,448	-7.4
Imports	164,916	159,786	-3.1
Total Trade	259,772	245,368	-5.5
Balance of Trade	-70,060	-74,204	

[*]Laos and Myanmar joined ASEAN on 23 July 1997 and Cambodia joined on 30 April 1999. Figures for these countries, therefore, are not included in the data.

TABLE 2: Summary of Hong Kong's Trade with Thailand

Volume in HK$ million

	July 96 – June 97	July 97 – June 98	% Change July – June 98/97
Domestic Exports	2,510	1,881	-25.1
Re-exports	12,080	11,154	-7.7
Imports	23,946	25,741	+7.5
Total Trade	38,536	38,776	+0.6
Balance of Trade	-9,356	-12,706	

(iii) A view from Thailand on Hong Kong's transition

Since 1 July 1997, the Hong Kong SAR has confronted many challenges, indeed, many more than most people had expected. Yet the Hong Kong administration deserves praise for its comparatively smooth implementation of the unique one country two systems model. Beijing should also be commended for its strict adherence to the spirit of the Basic Law. And the Hong Kong civil service has remained stable since the transition. During the World Bank/International Monetary Fund annual meetings held in Hong Kong in September 1997, finance ministers, financial market leaders and journalists from all over the world witnessed first-hand the smooth operation of Hong Kong since reunification.

Hong Kong's economy has been hard hit by fall out from the Asian financial crisis. GDP which grew by 5.5% in 1997, declined by around 2% in the first quarter of 1998 — the worst performance since 1985. Stock market capitalisation was down by 46% at the end of May 1998, compared with the peak in August 1997. Residential property prices dropped by 28% in April 1998, compared with the peak in October 1997. The Hong Kong dollar remained steady in the face of massive speculative attacks in August 1998, while the IMF fully supported Hong Kong's subsequent market intervention. Hong Kong has provided businesses and investors a haven of currency stability within a region in turmoil. Tourist arrivals in 1997 dropped 11.0% from 1996, declining a further 24% in the first 4 months of 1998 compared to the same period in 1997. However, with 10.4 million arrivals in 1997, Hong Kong was still the most popular tourist destination in Asia. Part of this success stems from its gateway status to China.

Media freedom continued with questions and criticism of government decisions in the context of as much openness as before the handover. Sensitive issues such as Tibet, Taiwan, and Mainland dissidents have been freely discussed. Controversial films such as *Seven Years in Tibet*, which was indirectly critical of the Mainland, continued to be screened in Hong Kong. Political protest was alive and well. More than 1,400 demonstrations — 140 a week compared to 87 a week one month before the handover — had taken place in the first ten months of the reunification. It was reported that police had not refused a single application for permits to march at the Annual Tiananmen Square vigil, held peacefully and without incident on June 4, 1998. Moreover, despite earlier concerns and criticism, elections for the first Legislative Council were held successfully on 4 May 1998 with a record number of candidates (166), registered voters (2.8 million) and actual voters (1.49 million) — a surprisingly robust voter turnout rate of 53%.

Hong Kong has remained one of the world's safest cities. The crime rate in 1997 was the lowest in 24 years with the downward trend continuing throughout 1998. The Independent Commission Against Corruption, meanwhile, has maintained its stringent world renowned vigil against unacceptable practices in the private and public sectors. The pre-handover prediction of a sharp rise in corruption was unfounded. Migration dropped 23% in 1997 to 30,000, compared to 40,300 in 1996 and a peak of 66,200 in 1992. The net inflow of Hong Kong residents doubled in 1997 to 127,000 compared to 63,900 in 1996. There has been steady increase in the expatriate population (excluding foreign domestic helpers) rising from 200,000 at the end of 1993 to 335,000 at the end of 1997. The Hong Kong SAR was also forced to cope with an outbreak of a deadly avian flu virus and a polution related "red tide" event which devestated a large number of local fish farms. In both cases the administration responded swiftly and decisively. Taken together, all these circumstances and trends strongly suggest that the Hong Kong SAR has so far kept things under control in the face of many challenges.

Prospects for Complimentarity and Cooperation between Hong Kong and Thailand

Southeast Asia views Hong Kong as the southeastern gateway to China. However, the rapid pace of economic development in the vast Chinese hinterland will pose an array of challenges to Hong Kong's physical and other infrastructure. Mainland Southeast Asia offers a logical alternative gateway to Southwestern China through Yunnan, Guangxi, and Sichuan provinces. The 500 million people in ten ASEAN nations, plus nearly 1.3 billion people in each of China and South Asia, with rapidly rising incomes should be perceived as a gigantic and growing market now and into the 21st Century.

This market is in the process of being linked internally and to the rest of the world by the grand 2-1-2 projects. The first "2" refers to two international rivers. The first is the Lancang Jiang in China which becomes the Mekong in Myanmar, Laos, and Thailand flowing from China's Yunnan Province along the Thailand-Laos border and through Cambodia and Vietnam into the South China Sea. The second is the Nujiang which flows from the southwestern part of Yunnan Province into Myanmar where it becomes the Salween River flowing along part of Thailand's western border with Myanmar before flowing into the Andaman Sea. The "1" refers to a system of Asian and European railways which will link up Southeast Asia with the Chinese railway system in Yunnan or Guangxi Provinces and via the Trans-Siberian railway to Amsterdam. The last "2" refers to the Asian highways routes — A-1 and A-2 — which are over 90% completed linking Southeast Asia and South Asia through Turkey with the network of European highways. When the A-1 and A-2 systems become linked to the Chinese network of highways via northern Thailand (a gap of only 230–260 km from the Thai province of Chiangmai to Yunnan Province), the whole of Asia will be linked with the European highways system.

When some or all of these five major projects are in operation, Southeast Asia — with Thailand as the focal point — will serve as the natural southwestern terrestrial gateway to China for Europe, the Middle East, Africa, South Asia, Southeast Asia and, to some extent, Australia by reducing the considerable time and costs in transportation. While the current financial crisis may have set back the clock for some time, the 2-1-2 scheme will again soon draw the attention of the world. Hong Kong with its experience and expertise as the southeastern gateway to China may participate in the joint investments for these five grand projects, thus bringing East and Southeast Asia to a new stage of prosperity.

As a greatly interested neighbouring country, Thailand maintains a close watch on the Hong Kong SAR. We share the same destiny and, with our other neighbours in the region, must face similar challenges. Thailand and Hong Kong have experienced years of high property prices, high growth rates, high inflation, and high wage increases — especially in Hong Kong — all of which have an impact on competitiveness. The financial meltdown has accelerated the pace of the necessary and painful changes. Since the Hong Kong economy is more robust than that of Thailand such changes will be less traumatic. In this context, with almost ten times the population of Hong Kong and 530 times its land area, Thailand's strong agro-based industries, advanced agricultural technology, strategic geographical location, and low-wages provide a set of complementary opportunities to the economy of Hong Kong.

Conclusion

The optimistic view of Hong Kong's future is based upon the SAR's remarkably resilient and flexible economy and workforce which is able to respond quickly and efficiently to the rapid changes in the regional and global marketplace. The SAR is well positioned regionally and globally under the rule of law, a well-managed, well-regulated economy and a clean and open administration. This is underpinned by the success of the one country two systems formula and the support of Beijing. Hong Kong seems to have the capacity and the track record to be among the first to take full advantage of the regional recovery when it comes. Moreover, sizable foreign reserves, a prudent fiscal policy and low, predictable taxes will, in the mean time, provide the economy with the breathing space it needs during the current volatility.

On the other hand, a more pragmatic view of Hong Kong would perceive the relevant issues in a somewhat different light. Economic recovery alone will not cure Hong Kong of its weaknesses. The territory needs to rethink both the way it does business and the kind of business it does. Indeed, Hong Kong does not have to follow the rest of Asia in a declining economic spiral. It can and should use the present crisis to create new opportunities, upgrade its industries, and fix what is broken in its economic structure. Responding to the downturn that grips most of Asia, but also reinventing itself for future growth, will be relatively easy for Hong Kong given its relative strength.

Several courses of action may be appropriate. First, it has to liberalise its economy further and to make it a less expensive city in Asia to do business. Hong Kong must take seriously concerns about the SAR's ability to manage its affairs. Such concerns were nowhere more clearly heightened than during the chaotic opening of the new US$20 billion Chek Lap Kok Airport in July 1998. Air freight shipments were disrupted for seven weeks, costing the Hong Kong economy nearly US$600 million or 0.35% of its GDP.

Second, it is time for Hong Kong to upgrade its manufacturing sector. Hong Kong has become prosperous shifting the production of toys, garments and watches into South China beginning in the late 1970s. However, the very low oparating costs in the PRC removed the incentive for the constant upgrading of businesses. Other traditional industries like garment manufacturing, for example, could generate more value added by creating fashion designs and high quality brand names rather than just merely farming out the production of cheap goods for the world's discount outlets.

Third, even the service sectors such as tourism could benefit from a restructuring. A sharp fall in tourist spending, which accounts for 10% of Hong Kong's GDP, has wiped out 20% of the SAR's 20,000 restaurants. High cost Hong Kong can no longer present itself as a shoppers' paradise. Moreover, Hong Kong needs to diversify from its focus on financial services, wherein the impact of an inevitable globalization is dulling its edge. Hong Kong has the potential to become a global leader in e-commerce applications, and in entertainment services including movies and computer games. Software and information services are demonstrated to have the highest returns on total investment. Hong Kong should think about shifting its emphasis to such industries.

Hong Kong has played a critical role in the far reaching changes in China since the Mainland opened its doors to the outside world. Now, as a special part of China, Hong Kong wants to continue to contribute to China's prosperity and stability. Hong Kong's apparent capacity to effectively respond to the challenges and opportunities posed by the handover and the recent crisis augurs well for the future of the entire region including Thailand.

Chapter 7
HONG KONG'S TRANSITION: A VIEW FROM THE SOUTH PACIFIC

Gerald CHAN[1]

"Hong Kong will remain one of the most open, free, exciting and cosmopolitan cities on earth."[2]

"It was not a question that we had abandoned our free-market principles."[3]

Sir Donald Tsang, Hong Kong's Financial Secretary

---

[1] I am grateful to my discussant, Dr. Shee Poon Kim formerly of the East Asian Institute, NUS, for his comments and suggestions. I also wish to thank Dr. P. K. Lee of the Hong Kong Open University, Dr. Jane Lee of the Hong Kong Policy Research Institute, Stephanie Lee of the New Zealand Consulate-General in Hong Kong, Dr. O. K. Lai of Waikato University, New Zealand, Pamela Barton of Asia 2000 Foundation of New Zealand, and my colleagues at Victoria University of Wellington: Bryce Harland, Peter Harris, Dr. Rod Alley, Dr. Tim Beal, Guy Reynolds, and Corinna deWolff, for their advice on the contents and sources for this chapter. I alone am responsible for the interpretations and shortcomings in this chapter.

[2] Donald Tsang, "Hong Kong: looking towards the future", speech made at the International Business Conference of the New South Wales State Chamber of Commerce, Sydney, Australia, on 25 August 1997. A full text can be found at <http://www.info.gov.hk/isd/speech/fs97825.htm>.

[3] *Asiaweek*, Hong Kong, 23 October 1998.

Introduction

Because of its cosmopolitan nature, Hong Kong's transition has global ramifications, especially in the economic arena, felt as far away as in the South Pacific. Like Asia itself, the South Pacific perspective on the transition is diverse, since the South Pacific covers a wide geographical area with diverse political, economic, and cultural systems. The major regional organisation in this area is the South Pacific Forum, which consists of 15 member countries: Australia; the Cook Islands; the Federated States of Micronesia; Fiji; Kiribati; Nauru; New Zealand; Niue; Papua New Guinea; the Republic of Marshall Islands; the Solomon Islands; Tonga; Tuvalu; Vanuatu; and Western Samoa. Of these, Australia and New Zealand stand out as first among equals because of their political and economic powers and their international standing. Australia and New Zealand each contribute one quarter of the annual budget of the Forum and offer substantial amounts of aid to fellow members. Their voices carry more weight in the decision-making process in the Forum, although decisions are customarily made by consensus based on the so-called "Pacific Way".[4]

Therefore, this chapter will concentrate on the views of Australia and New Zealand on Hong Kong's transition to Chinese sovereignty. The Australian and New Zealand views can be roughly divided into governmental and non-governmental perspectives. It is comparatively easier to gather governmental views rather than non-governmental views since the latter are too diverse to constitute any clear-cut thrust and hence any major policy impact as far as foreign affairs are concerned. Consequently, this chapter will focus on the official governmental views.

---

[4] Michael Haas, *The Pacific Way: Regional Cooperation in the South Pacific* (New York: Praeger, 1989).

Because of historical, constitutional, and cultural links with Britain, Australia and New Zealand are often regarded as belonging to the West. However, with the economic rise of Asia in the past two decades and the geographic proximity between Asia and the South Pacific, both Australia and New Zealand are giving increasing attention to developing better relations with their Asian neighbors, in the areas of trade, politics, security, and migration.[5] Both are in a continuous process of assessing and reassessing their national identities, especially in terms of whether or not they are more Asian. Obviously, the future of China and the future of Hong Kong are matters of great concern to policy-makers in both countries.

Although Australia and New Zealand are often lumped together with the Western liberal democratic camp, they differ from each other in some significant ways. For example, they have different parliamentary structures and different security policies towards the United States. Unlike Australia, New Zealand has so far maintained steadfastly its policy of no-nuclear-ship visits to the country. Although the two have entered into Closer Economic Relations and Closer Defence Relations, they often quarrel with each other over some bilateral economic issues and compete fiercely with each other in the sporting field. On balance, however, they have more in common than there are differences, and it is not unreasonable to consider them together at a higher level of analysis.

Several themes run through this chapter, including trade, investments, tourism, and cultural exchanges. These belong to the area of low politics, as opposed to those belonging to high politics such as military strategy and defence. In the area of high politics,

---

[5] For some background reading, see Gerald Chan, "Australian and New Zealand perspectives on Asia-Pacific development", in K. S. Liao (ed.), *The New International Order in East Asia* (Hong Kong: Chinese University of Hong Kong, 1993), pp. 149–70.

there is no disputing the reversion of Hong Kong's sovereignty to China on the part of Australia and New Zealand. In fact, the Australian foreign minister, Alexander Downer, while attending the handover ceremonies in Hong Kong in July 1997, was quoted as saying that it was time to give Hong Kong a chance under Chinese sovereignty.[6] He also defended China's decision to send 4,000 People's Liberation Army troops into Hong Kong, saying that the transfer of sovereignty "means, among other things, that China has responsibility for the defence of Hong Kong and that it is something they will have to manage themselves."[7] His statement was in sharp contrast to the British Foreign Secretary Robin Cook, who said that the sending of troops was unnecessary and inappropriate.

Australian Policy Towards Hong Kong[8]

The Australian government has expressed the view that the extensive range of Australian interests in Hong Kong will be best served by the maintenance of Hong Kong's stability and prosperity. Central to such stability and prosperity is the preservation of a high degree of autonomy for the Hong Kong Special Administrative Region (SAR) and the continuation of those elements of Hong Kong's way of life that have underpinned its success: the rule of law; the free flow of information, labour and capital; and all the rights and freedoms the people of Hong Kong currently enjoy. However, the issue of Hong Kong is intimately connected with Australia's greater, more important relations with China, a relationship which has implications for

---

[6] *The Age*, Melbourne, 3 July 1997. The opposition Labour Party had previously put pressure on Downer not to attend the handover ceremonies. See *The Age*, 13 June 1997.

[7] *The Age*, 30 June 1997.

[8] The following narrative of Australia's relations with Hong Kong is taken from <http://www.dfat.gov.au/geo/na/hongkong_brief.html>.

Australia's relationships with other powers in the region, in particular the United States. Balancing the demands of the Australia–China relationship against the interests of the people of Hong Kong will present unique problems for Australian foreign policy.[9]

In a broad political economic context, Australia and New Zealand supported Hong Kong's accession to the General Agreement of Tariffs and Trade as a separate contracting party in 1985 and its membership of the Pacific Economic Cooperation Council in 1990. More importantly, Australia played a role in having Hong Kong, along with China and Taiwan, granted entry into the Asia-Pacific Economic Cooperation (APEC) forum in 1991 on the basis that APEC was a group of 'economies' rather than states.

Trade

To Australia, Hong Kong is the most visible and symbolically important business beach-head in Asia. It is where the China trade starts.[10] The Australian Chamber of Commerce (AustCham), formed in 1987 to promote and develop business, trade, investment, services and goodwill between Australia, Hong Kong and the People's Republic of China, is the largest Australian chamber outside Australia and the second largest (after the U.S.) and most active international chamber in Hong Kong, reflecting the growing strength of Australian business in "Greater China" (Hong Kong, Taiwan, and mainland China). Over the last ten years AustCham has grown to over 1,000 members and it currently represents almost 500 Australian companies, employing around 10,000 people in Hong Kong.

---

[9] Stephen Sherlock, 'Hong Kong and the transfer to China: Issues and prospects,' Current Issue Brief No. 33, Department of the Parliamentary Library, Canberra, 23 June 1997, pp. 17–18.

[10] *The Australian*, 24 October 1997.

Hong Kong is Australia's eleventh largest trading partner. Australia's merchandise exports to Hong Kong in 1997 totalled A$3.8 billion and two-way merchandise trade stood at A$4.8 billion. As such, Australia benefits immensely in its trade with Hong Kong (see Tables 1 and 2 for details). In 1995–96, Hong Kong was Australia's ninth largest market for the export of services worth A$759 million with tourism and education being important components. Both total trade and Australia's merchandise exports have grown at a rate of 5.7% per annum in the five years to 1996.[11] Since China embarked on its modernisation policy in 1978, Sino-Australian trade through Hong Kong has increased substantially. Re-exports of goods of Australian origin through Hong Kong to China increased by over 420% from HK$683 million (A$112.2 million) in 1990 to HK$3.6 billion (A$635.1 million) in 1995. Re-exports of goods of Chinese origin to Australia through Hong Kong increased by over 145% from HK$4.9 billion (A$803.9 million) to HK$12 billion (A$2 billion) over the same period.[12] In 1996 about A$3.1 billion, or 47.2%, of mainland China-Australia trade went through the territory.[13]

For New Zealand, Hong Kong was the ninth largest trading partner,[14] and sixth largest export market in the world (fourth largest in the Asia Pacific region), absorbing HK$3,160 million (NZ$625 million) or 3.1% of New Zealand's total domestic exports by value in 1995. The value of Hong Kong's total 1995 imports

---

[11] In 1996, exports included unprocessed primary products (seafood, wool, coal, fruit and nuts – 22.3% of total exports), processed primary products (meat, milk products – 9.1%), simply transformed manufactures (pearls and precious stones, aluminium – 16.3%), elaborately transformed manufactures (medicines, plastics, photographic supplies, office machines and computers – 39.7%) and other products including gold (12.5%). Some 31% of Australia's exports are estimated to be re-exported to China.
[12] <http://www.info.gov.hk/info/austj.htm>, p. 1.
[13] *Ibid.*
[14] <http://www.info.gov.hk/trade/commercial/new_zeal.htm>.

from New Zealand, including retained imports and subsequent re-exports, reached HK$3,336 million (NZ$660 million), up 23.9% over the previous year. For the year to April 1998, New Zealand's exports to Hong Kong went up 4.8%.[15] New Zealand supplies a variety of very important raw materials and basic consumer goods to Hong Kong (See Table 3). For the year ending May 1997, New Zealand's exports to Hong Kong amounted to NZ$572.6 million, which was about 7.6% of its total exports to Asia that year and about 2.7% of its total world exports. The bulk of exports consisted of fish (NZ$87 million), fruit ($69 million), wood ($57 million), and paper ($30 million).[16] New Zealand imported merchandise from Hong Kong worth HK$1,151 million (NZ$228 million) in 1995, accounting for 1.1% of New Zealand's total imports. Hong Kong ranked as New Zealand's 18th largest importer that same year. Hong Kong is a major supplier of many very important intermediate goods and light consumer products for New Zealand (see Table 4).

As an important regional *entrêpot*, Hong Kong plays a key role in facilitating trade between New Zealand and other countries in the Asia Pacific region. In 1995 New Zealand products worth HK$1,222 million (NZ$242 million) were re-exported through Hong Kong to third markets, and goods valued at HK$2,155 million (NZ$426 million) were re-exported to New Zealand through Hong Kong from various sources. As the gateway to China, Hong Kong is an important bridge for Sino-New Zealand trade. Indirect trade between New Zealand and China through Hong Kong increased by four times from HK$723 million (NZ$157 million) in 1990 to HK$2,979 million (NZ$589 million) in 1995.

---

[15] 'Hong Kong in May/June 1998', New Zealand Consulate-General, Hong Kong, p. 2.

[16] Richard Amor et al., "In the forest of the night: second report of the Asian economic crisis monitoring group", Discussion paper No. 52, Commerce Division, Lincoln University, New Zealand, July 1998, pp. 4–5.

TABLE 1: Australian Exports to Hong Kong, 1994/95

Product	Rank among Australia's export markets (1994/95)	Value ($million)
Crustaceans and molluscs	2	HK$987 (A$172)
Pearls and precious stones	2	HK$778 (A$136)
Copper	5	HK$432 (A$75)
Zinc	2	HK$421 (A$73)
Photographic and cinematographic supplies	2	HK$419 (A$73)
Medicaments (including veterinary)	3	HK$324 (A$57)
Computers	2	HK$311 (A$54)

TABLE 2: Hong Kong Exports to Australia, 1994/95

Product	Rank among Australia's export markets (1994/95)	Value ($million)
Computers	5	HK$743.2 (A$129.7)
Cathode valves and tables, etc.	4	HK$644.6 (A$112.5)
Parts for office machines and computer	5	HK$625.1 (A$109.1)
Printed matter	3	HK$367.9 (A$64.2)
Woven cotton fabrics	5	HK$138.1 (A$24.1)
Clothing, of textile fabrics	3	HK$97.4 (A$17.0)

Notes: A$1=HK$5.73 (1995) (approximate average rate);
A$1=HK$5.66 (1994) (approximate average rate)

Source: <http://www.info.gov.hk/trade/commercial/australia.htm>, pp. 1–2.

TABLE 3: New Zealand Exports to Hong Kong, 1995

Product	Rank among (Percentage of) HK's import markets	Value ($million)
Degreased, non carbonised wool	1 (73.1%)	HK$410 (NZ$81)
Butter	1 (61.1%)	HK$151 (NZ$30)
Frozen fish fillets	2 (18.2%)	HK$118 (NZ$23)
Prepared or preserved molluscs	3 (17.8%)	HK$86 (NZ$17)
Concentrated milk	1 (54.2%)	HK$84 (NZ$17)

TABLE 4: Hong Kong exports to New Zealand, 1995

Product	Value ($million)
Electrical equipment	HK$263 (NZ$52)
Machinery	HK$186 (NZ$37)
Textiles and fabrics	HK$136 (NZ$27)
Clothing	HK$95 (NZ$19)
Printed matter	HK$88 (NZ$17)
Optical, photographic and medical equipment	HK$45 (NZ$9)
Watches and clocks	HK$37 (NZ$7)
Toys and dolls	HK$27 (NZ$5)

Note: NZ$1=HK$5.056 (1995 approximate average rate)
Source: <http://www.info.gov.hk/trade/commercial/new_zeal.htm>

Investments

Hong Kong is Australia's fifth largest destination for foreign investment, with total investment amounting to A$6.6 billion as of 30 June 1996. Australia's investments cover projects in a number of industries including insurance, services, trading, steel fabrication, concrete supply and quarrying, building, road construction, telecommunications and banking. About 320 Australian companies have established offices in Hong Kong.[17] Major Australian investors there include Broken Hill Proprietary, Carlton & United Breweries Limited, National Mutual, and Australia's "big four" banks.[18] About A$2 billion of the investment money that ploughed into Hong Kong is primarily to service the booming trade in South China.[19]

On the other hand, Hong Kong is the fourth largest source of foreign investment in Australia with total investment amounting to HK$76.4 billion (A$13.3 billion) as at 30 June 1996. A large proportion of this investment comes from the steady stream of small enterprises who have made Australia their home,[20] and is concentrated in real estate and the financial sector. Only 7.7% of accumulated Hong Kong investment in Australia is direct investment. Major Hong Kong investors in Australia include Jardine Pacific, Dairy Farm, Hutchison Whampoa, New World Development, and Swires. Both the Hong Kong Bank and the Standard Chartered Bank have substantial operations in Australia with branches and subsidiaries in many major cities.

Prominent New Zealand companies in Hong Kong include Fletcher Construction, Brierley Investments, New Zealand Milk Products, Air New Zealand, Forestry Corporation of New Zealand, and Lion Nathan Investments. The New Zealand Meat Producers Board, the New Zealand Kiwifruit Marketing Board, and the New Zealand Tourism Board all have offices in Hong Kong. The New Zealand Trade Development Board and the New Zealand–Hong Kong Business Association, the latter having a 250-strong membership, help to promote trade between Hong Kong, New Zealand, and

---

[17] <http://www.info.gov.hk/trade/commercial/australia.htm>, p. 2.
[18] Namely: National Australia Bank, Australia and New Zealand Banking Group, Commonwealth Bank of Australia, and Westpac Banking Group.
[19] *The Australian*, 24 October 1997, p. 2.
[20] *Ibid.*

China. In the financial sector, New Zealand banks and financial institutions operating in Hong Kong include the Australia and New Zealand Banking Group and New Zealand Insurance. The National Bank of New Zealand also has a representative office in Hong Kong, while the Hong Kong Bank has offices in Auckland and Wellington.

Market Opportunities for Infrastructure Projects

Priority sectors for Australian investments in Hong Kong include the building and construction infrastructure projects, processed foodstuffs and fresh foods and beverages, hides, skins and leather, environmental management and pollution control, marine and rail transport, telecommunications and information industries, consumer products and services (including education), and off-shore banking and professional services (including legal and medical). Australian companies have won contracts valued at more than HK$8.6 billion ($A1.5 billion) across a wide range of industrial sectors. Some of the Australian companies which have won contracts include EBC Hassell for part of the Chek Lap Kok design master-plan, Connell Wagner for part of the terminal design, Leighton Asia for various projects, Roche Bros. for earthworks sub-contracts for airport site formation, Barclay Mowlem for airport railway track, Eltin Asia which is part of the North Lantau Expressway consortium, and Dyno Westfarmers and ICI Australia which have won explosives contracts. A New Zealand-led consortium won 3% of the Hong Kong airport contract.[21] Austrade is confident that Australian expertise in infrastructural engineering will help Australian companies

---

[21] Pansy Wong, a New Zealand Member of Parliament who came originally from Hong Kong, during a question-and-answer session with the Hong Kong SAR Chief Executive, Tung Chee-Hwa, in Auckland on 17 June 1998.

to win contracts in the proposed New Huadu International Airport, which will serve as a key hub for Chinese domestic air services, replacing Guangzhou's over-stressed Baiyun Airport.[22]

Services

Hong Kong is Australia's ninth largest market for the export of services worth A$759 million in 1995–96, up from A$624 million in 1994–95. Services exports have grown at around twelve% per annum in the five years to June 1995. Australian companies have achieved a good market share across all service sectors, especially accounting, consultancy, insurance, legal, and finance and banking.

In 1996, 153,200 Hong Kong tourists visited Australia, up from 132,000 in 1995.[23] Compared with other Asian markets, a large number of these visits were for business or to see friends and relatives, while a relatively small number were holiday visits. In turn Australia is Hong Kong's sixth largest source of visitors with 311,000 Australian tourists visiting Hong Kong in 1996, up from 280,000 in 1995. According to the Hong Kong Tourist Association,[24] visitor arrivals to the city in June 1998 fell by 5.4% compared with June 1997, reaching a total of 746,145. In July 1998 tourist arrivals rose for the first time since Hong Kong returned to Chinese rule, jumping 26.5% from the previous year at 832,664 visitors.[25] Arrivals from Australia, New Zealand, and other South Pacific countries went up by 23.9%, but this could hardly make up for the extended decline in visitors from Northeast and Southeast Asia as a result

---

[22] *The Australian*, 20 April 1998.
[23] Another source says that about 167,000 Hong Kong residents visited Australia in 1995, an increase of 13% over 1994.
[24] <http://www.hkta.org/thisweek/pr/visitors_0698.html>.
[25] *The Straits Times*, 22 August 1998, p. 21.

of the Asian financial crisis. The Hong Kong Tourist Association estimated that arrivals for the whole of 1998 would be down by about 6% from the previous year, with a total of less than 10 million visits.[26] During an official visit by Chief Executive Tung Chee-Hwa of the Hong Kong SAR to New Zealand in June 1998, an agreement was signed to waive visa requirements for Hong Kong SAR and British National (Overseas) passport holders to visit New Zealand for up to three months, effective on 1 October 1998. Both Tung and the New Zealand Prime Minister, Jenny Shipley, viewed this as an expression of confidence in Hong Kong.[27]

Hong Kong is Australia's largest source of full-fee, formal course students, with 11,150 Hong Kong students currently studying in Australia at secondary, tertiary and TAFE (Technical and Further Education) institutions and in English language courses, constituting about one-sixth of the total number of overseas students in Australia.[28] Australia enjoys a good academic reputation in Hong Kong and is regarded as competitive in cost terms. Australian educational institutions are also expanding distance education courses in Hong Kong, and promoting other specialised sectors such as management and trade courses. In 1997 there were 388 full-fee paying students from Hong Kong in secondary schools in New Zealand, 123 in polytechnics, and 215 in universities. The March

---

[26] <http://www.hkta.org/thisweek/pr/visitors_0698.html>.

[27] *Hong Kong Standard*, 19 June 1998; and 'Hong Kong in May/June 1998,' New Zealand Consulate-General, Hong Kong, p. 1. For further information about the relaxation of immigration rules to attract visitors and investors from Hong Kong to New Zealand, see *South China Morning Post*, Internet ed., 13 October 1998.

[28] <http://www.info.gov.hk/trade/commercial/australia.htm>, p. 3. For details of the growth of the number of Hong Kong students in Australia from 1989 to 1996, the sectoral breakdown, and the fields of study, see *Hong Kong: the transfer of sovereignty* ([Canberra]: Joint Standing Committee on Foreign Affairs, Defence and Trade, The Parliament of the Commonwealth of Australia, May 1997), pp. 108–109.

1998 figures show a drop of four students in secondary schools, but an increase of 23 in polytechnics and seven in universities when compared with a year earlier.[29]

Migration and Visitors

The strong socio-economic ties between Hong Kong, Australia and New Zealand also works in the other direction. About 30,000 Australian citizens are resident in Hong Kong, probably comprising Australia's largest expatriate group anywhere in the world.[30] In addition there are at least 2,000 holders of Australian permanent residency living in Hong Kong.[31] Australia is one of the top three most popular destinations for Hong Kong emigrants. Currently, some 90,000 former Hong Kong residents are living in Australia. Migrant visa grants for individuals in Hong Kong totalled 7,018 in 1996/97, down 8.1% from the previous year.[32] About 3,200 New Zealanders are living in Hong Kong, representing the largest New Zealand expatriate community in Asia. The New Zealand Society of Hong Kong, formed in 1957, plays a key role in helping New Zealand expatriates in Hong Kong and in promoting contacts between New Zealanders living in Hong Kong and those people in the territory interested in the New Zealand way of life.

Over 310,000 Australian visitors entered Hong Kong in 1996, spending a total of A$33 million.[33] Since 1991/92 visitor applications from Hong Kong have increased. In 1995/96, 103,642 visitor visas

---

[29] Amor et al., "In the forests of the night", pp. 11, 14, and 16–17.
[30] <http://www.info.gov.hk/info/austj.htm>, p. 2.
[31] Sherlock, "Hong Kong and the transfer to China: issues and prospects", p. 18.
[32] For some details of migration flow and migrant characteristics, see *Hong Kong: The transfer of sovereignty*, pp. 112–114.
[33] <http://www.info.gov.hk/info/austj.htm>, p. 2.

were granted (an 18.4% increase on the previous year), while 1996/97 saw a further 2.8% increase with 106,614 visitor visas granted for the twelve month period. Australia grants Hong Kong SAR passport holders equally favorable access as British National (Overseas) passport holders as does New Zealand. In 1996 and 1997, immigration processing procedures were significantly streamlined to facilitate the entry of business people and tourists from Hong Kong to Australia. Innovations included the introduction of Agency Arrangements whereby major Hong Kong travel agents process visitor visas on behalf of the Australian Consulate General. Streamlining procedures for the entry of skilled and business people, under the Regional Headquarters Programme, is also assisting Hong Kong-based companies to relocate all or part of their operations to Australia.

However, since July 1997, applications to migrate to Australia and other Western countries have dropped to the lowest level in nearly a decade. In the case of Australia, this is partly attributable to the tightening of the rules of entry by imposing a more stringent English language test and partly to a stabile first few months of Chinese rule. An Australian immigration official in Hong Kong said that 3,047 people applied to migrate to Australia between January and September 1997, compared to 8,420 in the corresponding period in 1996. The number of visas issued, however, did not yet reflect the fall in applications: 3,637 approvals in the first nine months of 1997, compared to 3,802 in the corresponding period in 1996. Canada, the most popular destination for Hong Kong residents seeking the insurance of a foreign passport, recorded an even greater drop in applications. Canada received only 2,228 applications in the first eight months of 1997, compared to 11,370 for the whole of 1996.[34] In the twelve years to 1994/95, more than 73,000 Hong Kong people

---

[34] *The Australian*, 3 November 1997.

have become Australian residents and the Hong Kong-born population now exceeds 100,000.[35]

Hong Kong was the sixth largest source of immigrants to New Zealand in 1995. New Zealand approved 3,100 residence applications from Hong Kong, with the largest group being business immigrants. Business travel and tourism are expanding rapidly between the two places. In the same year, about 31,000 Hong Kong residents visited New Zealand, and Hong Kong received about 50,000 visitors from New Zealand.[36]

Government and Trading Representatives

In addition to the Australian Consulate General, which represents the Australian federal government in Hong Kong, several state governments including the Northern Territories, South Australia, Victoria, Western Australia, and Queensland have representative offices in Hong Kong. The Hong Kong–Australia Business Association, established in 1987, has six divisions in New South Wales, Victoria, Queensland, South Australia, Western Australia, and the Northern Territories. The Hong Kong–New Zealand Business Association, also set up in 1987, has a liaison office in Auckland, while Austrade has offices Hong Kong and Guangzhou. The Hong Kong government, in turn, established its Economic and Trade Office in Sydney in 1995, which also looks after businesses in New Zealand. The Hong Kong Trade Development Council has more than 50 offices in 34 countries, including one in Sydney.

The Pauline Hanson factor, which has raised some concerns and unease in Asia (as well as in Australia), is only a minor voice in Australian politics. Australian business and academic circles, together

---

[35] *The Australian*, 24 October 1997.
[36] <http://www.info.gov.hk/trade/commercial/new_zeal.htm>.

with the ruling Liberal Party and the main opposition Labour Party, are actively opposed to the rise of such extreme anti-Asian nationalistic sentiments. The Australian government is trying to detach its policy from the Hanson effect. In a media interview, the Australian foreign minister, Alexander Downer, said that "our government has a very obvious vested interest in beating down Pauline Hanson's support, but we have to work out how best to do that," commenting that Australia is a democracy.[37] In the Australian general election in October 1998, Hanson lost her seat in the Parliament. Subsequently she faced a revolt within her own One Nation Party.[38] There is no near equivalent of such a phenomenon in New Zealand.

Cooperation in Judicial Governance

The Hong Kong Basic Law guarantees, among other things, the independence of the Hong Kong judiciary. On 1 July 1997 the Hong Kong Court of Final Appeal was set up to replace the Judicial Committee of the Privy Council as the highest appellate court for Hong Kong. For the first time in history, the power of final adjudication was vested in the Hong Kong Special Administrative Region, signifying Hong Kong's status as an autonomous common law jurisdiction. In the words of the Secretary for Justice, Ms Elsie Leung, this newly established Court "is not bound by the precedents of [the] Privy Council, it is the fountain of new developments in the common law of Hong Kong."[39] When hearing appeals, the Court will have five judges, consisting of the Chief Justice, three permanent

---

[37] *Far Eastern Economic Review*, 13 August 1998, p. 29.
[38] *The Straits Times*, 29 October 1998, p. 13.
[39] Elsie Leung, "The rule of law and its operation in Hong Kong after reunification", *Policy Bulletin*, Hong Kong, No. 6 (July 1998), pp. 7–8.

judges, and one non-permanent judge or one judge from another common law jurisdiction selected by the Chief Justice and invited by the Court. The pool of judges from other common law jurisdictions is currently made up of six members, two each from the United Kingdom, Australia, and New Zealand.[40] In putting forward the appointments of these judges from other jurisdictions, the Secretary of Justice said that "their appointment will bring to the Hong Kong Court of Final Appeal a wealth of invaluable experience. Furthermore they will provide an important conduit between the Hong Kong Special Administrative Region and other common law jurisdictions."[41]

The United Kingdom, Australia, and New Zealand, "have close affinity with Hong Kong in terms of their laws, legal tradition and procedure, including appellate procedures."[42] Lord Cooke of Thorndon, a former president of the New Zealand Court of Appeal, joined Chief Justice Andrew Li and three local judges for the first session of the new Hong Kong SAR Court of Final Appeal on 18 December 1997.[43] The appointment of the two New Zealand members led a seasoned China observer in Wellington to say that for the first time in the history of Hong Kong, New Zealand has a direct interest

---

[40] The two members from Australia are Sir Anthony Mason, former Chief Justice of the High Court of Australia, and Sir Daryl Dawson, a judge of the High Court of Australia. The two members from New Zealand are Lord Cooke of Thorndon, former President of the Court of Appeal in New Zealand now siting in the House of Lords in England, and Sir Edward Somers, a former judge of the New Zealand Court of Appeal. See the speech by the Secretary for Justice, Ms Elsie Leung, in moving a resolution under the Hong Kong Court of Final Appeal Ordinance (Cap. 484) in the Provisional Legislative Council, 23 July 1997, at <http://www.info.gov.hk/isd/speech/723-just>.

[41] *Ibid.*, p. 4.

[42] *Ibid.*, p. 3.

[43] The case was a battle over the rights to a piece of land in the New Territories. See "Hong Kong in November/December 1997", New Zealand Consulate-General, Hong Kong, p. 2.

in the governance of Hong Kong,[44] although this involvement is apparently quite minimal.

Conclusion

Hong Kong, Australia, and New Zealand shared several common interests. First, they all have a big stake in the vitality of the Asian market: Australia's trade with "Greater China" accounted for eleven percent of its total trade in 1996; while eleven of Hong Kong's top twenty trading partners are in the Asia-Pacific Region. Second, they all have a common law system, a legacy of British colonial rule. Third, both Australia and New Zealand, together with most other countries in the world, recognise the attractiveness of Hong Kong's low level of taxation and its role as a service and *entrepôt* centre for trade with China. Fourth, the people-to-people relationships among the three have increased significantly in recent years due to migration and visits.[45]

Hong Kong remains crucial as a gateway and facilitator for Sino-Australian as well as Sino-New Zealand trade, although there are signs that such a role has diminished slightly in recent years. While Australia's trade with China has grown at about twenty percent a year since 1993, trade with Hong Kong has started to lag slightly behind that rate, suggesting that businesses can increasingly bypass the territory to deal directly with the mainland.[46] Politically, Australia

---

[44] Remark made by Bryce Harland, director of the New Zealand Institute of International Affairs, formerly ambassador to China and the UK, in a personal communication with Peter Harris, director of the Asian Studies Institute, Victoria University of Wellington, July 1998.

[45] The people-to-people relationship was stressed on a number of occasions by Chief Executive Tung Chee-Hwa in his Melbourne Forum address on 16 June 1998 and his press conference in Wellington on 18 June 1998 during his official visit to Australia and New Zealand.

[46] *The Australian*, 17 November 1997.

and New Zealand have maintained a low profile with respect to the territory's internal domestic disputes, adopting a low-key approach in the case of Australia and quiet diplomacy in the case of New Zealand.

The China factor in Australia's and New Zealand's policies towards Hong Kong is obvious, especially after the Cold War when economic matters assumed relatively greater importance than political and strategic affairs. Their policies towards China are, of course, very much influenced by America's policy towards China. It would be difficult to imagine, for example, that Australian and New Zealand human rights policies towards China would overshadow those of the United States in condemning human rights abuses in China. Now that the United States has embarked on a policy of "strategic partnership"[47] (or soft containment or neo-containment)[48] with China, there is little incentive for Australia and New Zealand to tread a diplomatic path independent of the United States. Furthermore, the increasing amount of freedom enjoyed by the Chinese people, China's willingness to continue to engage in human rights dialogues with other countries and international agencies, and its signing of the International Covenant on Civil and Political Rights in October 1998 mean that there is little cause for major conflict of polices and interest between China and Australia and New Zealand.

---

[47] In his visit to China in mid-1998, President Clinton spelt out clearly that the United States and China were entering into a relationship of strategic partnership.

[48] "Soft containment" was a concept used by Professor Immanuel C. Y. Hsu in his public lecture on 'Chinese American relations on the eve of the 21st Century' delivered in Singapore on 18 September 1998 to describe United States' policy towards China under the guise of "constructive engagement" and "strategic partnership". "Neo-containment", however, is a term used by Professor Alastair I. Johnston, "Engaging myths: misconceptions about China and its global role", *Harvard Asia Pacific Review*, Vol. 2, No. 1 (Winter 1997/98), pp. 9–12.

In the period since the handover, there has been no paradigm shift in terms of Hong Kong's political structure and its relations with China. Incremental changes in Hong Kong's political culture that would require fine adjustments in a more or less mechanical, step-by-step way are evident, however. Barring any major upheavals in international affairs and China's domestic situation, no fundamental changes are likely in Australian and New Zealand policies towards Hong Kong.

Appendix[49]

Recommendations made by the Joint Standing Committee on Foreign Affairs, Defence and Trade of The Parliament of the Commonwealth of Australia to the Australian government on the Hong Kong Special Administrative Region (HKSAR)

A. Relating to 'one country, two systems'

1. The Australian Government urge the Government of the HKSAR not to implement the decision of the Preparatory Committee to dissolve the three tiers of representative government elected throughout 1994–95, the Municipal Councils, the District Boards and the Legislative Council.

2. The Australian Government urge the Government of the HKSAR:

   a. to present for public comment, at the earliest possible date, an electoral law, based on the widest possible franchise, for a properly constituted, elected legislative council; and

---

[49] Taken from the "Government response to the report of the Joint Standing Committee on Foreign Affairs, Defence and Trade on Hong Kong: The transfer of sovereignty" [Canberra, 1997].

b. hold elections according to that law, as soon as possible after 1 July 1997.
3. Australian ministers and officials, through representations to the Chief Executive of the HKSAR, urge the continuation of Hong Kong's open way of life, the maintenance of the Bill of Rights and the rapid introduction of a fully and freely elected legislature.
4. The Australian Government maintain direct links between Australian authorities and the HKSAR Civil Service to promote its continued independence as guaranteed under the principle of 'one country, two systems' and defined in the Joint Declaration and the Basic Law.
5. The Attorney-General:
   a. having in mind concerns expressed to the Committee by Justice Dowd on behalf of the International Commission of Jurists, investigate the means by which serving judges in Australia might be included in the lists for panels of judges to serve in Hong Kong;
   b. write to the Courts in Australia asking them to consider favourably their response to a request from the Hong Kong Judicial Commission to participate in panels for the Court of Final Appeal, should that occur; and
   c. urge the legal profession in Australia to maintain its links with the legal profession in Hong Kong after 1 July 1997 through as many formal and informal channels as possible, including the exchange of judges.
6. The Australian Government urge the Government of the HKSAR to:
   a. adhere to the promise of judicial independence in the fullest sense as defined in Articles 2 and 85 of the Basic Law;

b. amend section 4(2) of the Court of Final Appeal Ordinance in order to confine the meaning of 'an act of state' to defence and foreign affairs; and

c. provide clarification on how Articles 19 (limitation of HKSAR judicial power over acts of state such as foreign and defence affairs) and 158 (the power of interpretation of the Standing Committee of the National People's Congress) might work in practice.

B. Relating to issues raised by the transfer

7. The Australian Government urge:

a. the Government of the PRC to ratify the International Covenant on Civil and Political Rights (ICCPR); and

b. the Government of the HKSAR and the Government of the PRC to continue to meet the reporting obligations of the former under Article 40 of the ICCPR.

8. The Australian Government support, in the appropriate UN forums, the continued consideration of the application of the ICCPR in Hong Kong through either reports from the HKSAR or, in the absence of such reports, from relevant non government organisations.

9. The Australian Government express to the Government of the HKSAR its concerns about proposed changes to the Bill of Rights Ordinance, the Boundary and Election Commission Ordinance, the Electoral Provisions Ordinance, the Societies Ordinance and the Public Order Ordinance.

10. The Australian Government urge the Government of the HKSAR to establish a Human Rights Commission and offer the technical assistance of the Australian Human Rights and Equal Opportunity Commission to that end.

11. The Australian Government:

a. promote with the Government of the HKSAR the value of retaining freedom of expression and association;
b. express its concern over the vague and broad nature of Article 23 (regarding subversion); and
c. monitor, and as necessary, make timely representations to the HKSAR administration if freedoms of the press, speech or assembly are at risk of being eroded.

12. The Australian Government encourage the Australian Council of Trade Unions, through its international branch to:
a. maintain contacts with unions in Hong Kong to monitor the continuing rights of association of workers in Hong Kong; and
b. make representations to the International Labour Organisation where it is perceived that these rights are being eroded.

13. The Australian Government, within its dialogue with the Government of the PRC on human rights matters, seek clarification of the role of, criteria for and procedures under which the People's Liberation Army will give assistance to the HKSAR for the maintenance of public order or for disaster relief under Article 14 of the Basic Law.

14. The Australian Government seek clarification from the Government of the HKSAR and the PRC on the question of right of abode, in particular on how the declaration of foreign nationality is to be implemented, and subsequently advice affected Australians of their position.

15. The Australian Government:
a. monitor the situation of the dissidents and other individuals at risk and as appropriate make representations on their behalf to the Government of the HKSAR; and

b. give special consideration to applications from known dissidents should any apply for asylum.
16. The Australian Government:
a. encourage the Government of Vietnam to devote additional resources to providing clearances for the Vietnamese who remain in Hong Kong;
b. urge the administration of the HKSAR to regulate the status of asylum seekers who remain;
c. give consideration to assisting those in the residual population who have links to Australia through the provision of humanitarian resettlement if the position of those people in Hong Kong deteriorates to the point where their rights are being violated; and
d. support a role for UNHCR in monitoring the residual screened out population.
17. The Australian Government:
a. urge the Government of the United Kingdom to accept responsibility for the residual screened-in refugees and determine resettlement places for them prior to the transfer;
b. urge the Government of the HKSAR to assume responsibility for some of the residual refugees;
c. urge UNHCR to play an active role in monitoring the welfare of these people should they remain in the territory; and
d. reconsider any cases who have links to Australia that have been previously rejected for resettlement.
C. Relating to the Hong Kong economy:
18. The Australian Government include in its annual report on Hong Kong to the Parliament comment on the continued effective operation of the ICAC.

19. The Australian Government continue to support, both multilaterally and bilaterally, the accession of the PRC to the World Trade Organisation as a means to encourage the development of a consistent, transparent framework of rules and procedures for trade and commercial activity within the sovereign territory of China.

20. The Australian Government:
    a. maintain the presence in Hong Kong of its broadcast and broadband media, Australian Television and Radio Australia — in short wave and via satellite with services in Mandarin and Cantonese, as an available source of independent news, analysis and information on political, social and economic development in the region; and
    b. encourage private media concerns, including newsprint, radio and television broadcasters, to maintain their presence in Hong Kong as a means of encouraging continued international scrutiny of China's implementation of and adherence to the provisions and requirements of the Basic Law.

21. The Australian Government:
    a. maintain direct links with the Government of the HKSAR to reinforce the status of the territory as largely autonomous, with executive, legislative and independent judicial authority as provided for under the Basic Law;
    b. support, multilaterally and bilaterally, the continuing participation of the HKSAR as a separate entity in international trade agreements such as the WTO and APEC, further reinforcing its status as a largely autonomous territory.

22. On the establishment of an elected legislature in Hong Kong, the Joint Standing Committee on Foreign Affairs, Defence and

Trade seek to establish links with a counterpart committee in that legislature.

D. Relating to Australian interests

23. In the light of the importance of the education and training market in Hong Kong to Australia, the Australian Government urge the Government of the HKSAR to maintain its current visa arrangements for students from Hong Kong wishing to study in Australia.

24. On an annual basis, for at least the next five years, the Australian Government provide a report to the Parliament, having in mind the terms of the Joint Declaration and the Basic Law, on the political, economic and human rights developments in the HKSAR.

25. The Australian Government encourage the Government of the United Kingdom and the Government of the PRC to observe their treaty obligations in respect of Hong Kong under the Joint Declaration for the stipulated period of 50 years.

26. The Australian Government encourage the Government of the People's Republic of China to ratify the two major human rights covenants, the International Covenant on Civil and Political Rights and the International Covenant on Economic, Social and Cultural Rights.

ABOUT THE CONTRIBUTORS

Dr Gerald CHAN
Senior Lecturer of International Relations, Department of Politics, Victoria University of Wellington, New Zealand. Dr Chan was a Visiting Research Fellow in the East Asian Institute, National University of Singapore from 1 July to 31 December, 1998

Professor GAO Shangquan
Beijing University, The People's Republic of China; President, China Society for Enterprise Reform and Development

Dr LUO Qi
Research Fellow, East Asian Institute, National University of Singapore

Dr Stephen Leong
Assistant Director General, Institute of Strategic and International Studies, Kuala Lumpur, Malaysia

Dr Andrew M. MARTON
Research Fellow, East Asian Institute, National University of Singapore

Professor UMPHON Phanachet
Director, Chinese Studies Centre, Institute of Asian Studies, Chulalongkorn University, Bangkok, Thailand

Dr Jusuf WANANDI
Chairman and Member of the Supervisory Board, Centre for Strategic and International Studies, Jakarta, Indonesia

Dr Milton D. YEH
Research Fellow, Institute of International Relations, National Chengchi University, Taiwan, The Republic of China